NUTRITIOUS BROWN BAG LUNCHES

Margaret E. Happel

The Brethren Press
Elgin, Illinois

NUTRITIOUS BROWN BAG LUNCHES

Copyright © 1984 by Brethren Press

All rights reserved. No part of this book may be reproduced in any form without written permission from the publisher, except by a reviewer who wishes to quote brief passages in connection with a review in a magazine or newspaper.

The Brethren Press, 1451 Dundee Avenue, Elgin, IL 60120

Edited by Leslie R. Keylock

Library of Congress Catalog Number 84-071412

Printed in the United States of America

ISBN 0-87178-616-8

CONTENTS

Introducing the Nutritious Brown Bag Lunch	5
1. Savory Soups and Satisfying Stews	15
2. Sandwiches, Sandwiches, Sandwiches	33
3. Super Sandwiches	43
4. Finger-Lickin' Food	57
5. The Big Main-Dish Salad	69
6. Single-Serving Salads	85
7. Quick Muffins and Breads	95
8. Light Fruit Desserts	109
9. Cookies: A Sometimes Sweet Treat	125
10. "Go-Power" Super Snacks	133
11. Quick Nutrition "Fix-Its" for the Brown Bag Lunch	143
12. Lunch Box Menus	149
Index	155

INTRODUCING THE NUTRITIOUS BROWN BAG LUNCH

Why a guide to preparing nutritious brown bag lunches? We only have to be aware that over eighty million Americans carry their lunch to work every day. The brown bag lunch is not only here to stay—it is an expanding two-billion-meal-a-year phenomenon. At the office, at the factory, at school, more people than ever before open, eat, and enjoy a portable lunch—one that has invariably been made and packed the night before.

Despite the increase in fast-food franchises, local delicatessens, and in-plant cafeterias, the brown bag lunch habit booms. Budget and convenience may seem the obvious reasons, but for growing numbers of people the real impetus is nutrition.

In voting nutrition into their lunch bags, people are voting many of the prepared, store-bought lunch items out. A generation of nutritionally-aware consumers is saying "no" to a variety of products that form the core of a fourteen-billion dollar business focused around America's brown bag lunch habit.

Brown baggers love to control how much they eat and what they eat, particularly those brown baggers on any kind of diet. By making your own lunch (or for mothers who prepare lunch for their school-age kids) it is possible to guard against eating the nutritional "no-no's" of saturated fat, too much salt, and too much sugar. For serious dieters it is much easier to pack a prepared-ahead, calorie-controlled portion of a meal than to select from among the temptations of an "eating out" situation. For mothers it is a subtle yet effective way of programming sensible nutrition into children's lunches and programming out the junk foods invariably found in most school snack dispensing machines.

Thus, our guide to nutritious brown bag lunches is based on practical, possible food purchases and preparation habits. Wise buying at the supermarket can mean easy selection of nutritious foods. A little essential information guides you toward good purchases and away from bad ones. And it is an advantage to know that certain convenience foods have a place within today's lunch box.

Above all, this is a guide to persuade you that nutritious brown bag meals are not only delicious but also easily and simply made. Most recommendations are for "do ahead" storage overnight in the refrigerator. Some menus can be frozen and then thawed as needed. All are prepared with an eye to the nutritional wisdom of reducing the sugar, salt, and fat content of your diet while increasing the fiber and complex carbohydrate content of what you eat—that is, having more fresh fruit and vegetables and more grains and cereals in your meals.

There are some lunch box favorites that always have appeal and, fortunately, make good nutritional sense: peanut butter and jelly sandwiches for one, though it is best on whole wheat bread. And the jelly is sugar-reduced and with high vitamin C or vitamin A content. There are selections for all of us who prudently, from time to time, count calories and watch our weight. (People with more specialized and specific diet needs are strongly advised to follow a diet program devised by a physician and nutrition counselor, selecting foods for brown bagging from those that are easily and safely portable.)

And before you begin to pack your brown bag lunch, give attention to the special sections that guide you to the best equipment and emphasize the basic rules of safe food preparation. The meal you carry must be not only delicious, but also safeguarded against spoilage.

Above all, become familiar with our comprehensive nutrition guide, which enables you to make an easy and diverse selection of essential foods. Good nutrition and good health go hand-in-hand, even in a brown bag lunch.

A BASIC GUIDE TO BROWN BAG NUTRITION:

A delicious and sensible lunch should contain foods from all basic food groups. Nutritionists at the United States Department of Agriculture have devised these four groups to help people select food simply, in a balanced fashion, and in a way that will meet their recommended daily allowances (RDAs).

Lunch should not be skipped; it should not be a small meal. Your lunch should contain approximately one-third the volume of food eaten during the day. We need energy to continue working during the afternoon. And it is nutritionally unwise for us to eat a heavy meal at the end of the day to compensate for an inadequate breakfast and a meager midday meal.

Learn the four basic food groups, and make sure your lunch box contains a portion from each one. These recommendations are based on minimum servings for adults.

INTRODUCTION 7

- **THE MILK GROUP:** An essential source of calcium and a valuable source of protein, riboflavin (vitamin B_2), and vitamins A and D. People concerned with lowering the fat content of their diet should select low-fat milk (but one fortified with vitamins A and D) and skim-milk cheese.

  Foods to Select From: Whole milk, skim or low-fat milk, buttermilk, reconstituted nonfat dry milk, cocoa or chocolate-flavored malt drink, malted milk, whole-milk or skim-milk yogurt or yogurt with fruit added; skim- or whole-milk cheeses, white or low-fat cottage cheeses, ice cream or ice milk.

  Minimum Portions to Serve: The lunch box should contain one of the following: 1 cup (8 ounces) fluid milk products, yogurt, and milk-based products; 1/2 cup ice milk, ice cream, or cottage cheese products; 1 (1-ounce) slice firm or semisoft cheeses.

  Note: Nondairy creamers or whipped toppings are not dairy products, nor are sandwich spreads, ice cream, or desserts made from a "tofu," soybean base.

- **THE MEAT GROUP:** An essential source of protein, vitamin B complex, and iron. Meat can bring saturated fat and cholesterol to the diet. It is wise to choose "lean" meat—preferably chicken, other poultry, or fish.

  Foods to Select From: Meats, poultry, fish, cheese, eggs, and legumes, such as dried peas, beans, and nuts.

  Minimum Portions to Serve: The lunch box should contain one of the following:
  —2-3 ounces of poultry, not including skin and bone;
  for example: 1 chicken leg or thigh
                1 small deboned chicken breast
                2 (4 1/4 2 1/2 inches) slices any poultry
  —2-3 ounces of any meat, not including skin, fat, and bone:
  for example: 1 (3 1/4 1 1/2 inches) hamburger patty
                2 (4 1/4 2 1/2 inches) slices any lean meat
                1 (3/4-inch thick) lamb or pork chop, well trimmed
  —2-3 ounces of any fish, not including skin and bone:
  for example: 1/2 cup cooked, flaked shellfish
                1/3 cup canned fish, well drained
                4 fish sticks
  —2-3 ounces of cheese and eggs:

for example: ½ cup cottage cottage cheese
  2 slices (1 ounce each) firm or semisoft cheese
  2 eggs
—2-3 ounces of legumes (peas, beans, nuts):
for example: 1 cup cooked, diced peas or beans
  ½ cup nutmeats
  ¼ cup peanut butter
  ¼ cup or 2 ounces soybean protein, i.e., tofu

Note: To the person new to nutrition, it may be surprising that included in the Meat Group are cheese, eggs, and legumes (dried peas, beans and nuts). These foods, too, are valuable sources of protein and vitamin B complex, though it should be understood that cheese is not a good source of iron.

- **THE FRUIT AND VEGETABLE GROUP:** An essential source of vitamins A and C, plus an important source of minerals, fiber, and carbohydrates.

Foods to Select From: All fruits and fruit juices, salad vegetables, and prepared vegetables from the list below that indicate vitamin value.

Minimum Portions to Serve: The lunch box should contain a portion of fruit and a portion of vegetable in the following amounts:
  1 cup sliced, fresh fruit, unsweetened
  ¾ cup (6 fluid ounces) unsweetened fruit juice
  1 cup raw salad vegetable, not including dressing
  ½ cup cooked fruit or vegetable

Most importantly, select fruits and vegetables that add vitamin A and vitamin C to the diet.

Vitamin A Rich Fruits and Vegetables

Apricots	Carrots	Spinach
Cantaloupe	Collards	Sweet Potato
Papayas	Kale	Turnip Spears
Peaches	Mustard Greens	Winter Squash
Prunes	Pumpkin	

Vitamin C Rich Fruits and Vegetables

Beet Greens	Kale	Strawberries
Brussel Sprouts	Lemons	Tomatoes
Broccoli	Oranges	
Cantaloupe	Papayas	
Grapefruit	Peppers (green)	

Note: While the above list steers you to essential choices in your fruit and vegetable selection, do not omit other varieties. They, too, will provide vitamins (though in lesser amounts), essential minerals, and fiber.

- **BREAD AND CEREAL GROUP:** An essential source of carbohydrates, protein, vitamin B complex, and iron.

  Foods to Select From: Breads (especially those containing whole grain), cooked cereal, unsweetened ready-to-eat cereal (especially those made from whole grain), pastas, noodles, and spaghetti (made from enriched flour).

  Minimim Portions to Serve: The lunch box should contain two of the following, or a double portion of one:
  - 1 slice bread, preferably whole grain
  - 1 biscuit, roll or muffin, preferably whole grain or made from enriched flour
  - *1/2-3/4 cup cooked cereal or rice
  - *1 cup ready-to-eat cereal
  - 1/2-3/4 cup cooked pasta, noodles, or macaroni, made from enriched flour.

  *Not generally used in lunch boxes, but good to know.

  Note: Many people think of this group of foods as fattening and are tempted to omit them from their lunch box. However, carbohydrates are the body's chief source of energy. Omission will create an unbalanced diet and cause the incomplete digestion of other essential nutrients. Remember, unrefined carbohydrates (whole grains and enriched flours) contain valuable sources of vitamin B complex, iron, and fiber.

  Other Good Nutrition Points
- No single food is fattening. Only when you eat too much in relation to the energy you expend is food fattening.
- Food packed in a lunch box does not have to be eaten all at once. If carefully selected, with a thought to food safety, this portable food can be designed to be eaten as two or three snacks throughout the day. This is a better way for some people to satisfy their appetite and produce a constant energy level.

BUYING THE BEST OF THE LUNCH BOXES:
Brown bags are the device we automatically think of for packing lunches, but they are not the safest nor the best thing in which to carry food. While teenagers love to tote their lunches in brown bags as a cool status symbol, it is the little kids with their insulated cartoon-

character lunch boxes who have the best and most safely packed meals.

For health and safety reasons, discard the brown paper bag and make a selection from one of the following:

- Vacuum Bottles for hot and cold liquids (not carbonated beverages).
  - Select a narrow, standard-neck vacuum bottle. Buy non-breakable, non glass-lined bottles for children. Special pouring devices built into the vacuum bottle tops also help to dispense liquids safely.
  - For safety's sake, never drink directly from the neck of the bottle; never use the bottle for carrying carbonated beverages (it may shatter); and never use it to carry ice cubes. Secure firmly once filled.
- Wide-mouth Vacuum Bottles and Jars for hot and cold foods such as soups, stews, and finely-divided main-dish salads and fruit salads.
  - Select size according to need (this ranges from an 8-ounce bottle to a 1-quart size). Most come with a plastic liner to protect the glass interior.
  - For safety's sake preheat or prechill the bottle, depending on the type of food to be packed. Before packing superhot foods, fill the container with hot (not boiling) water and let stand ten minutes before draining and filling. Before filling with cold food, chill the open bottle and its top in the refrigerator for at least fifteen minutes, if not overnight. Secure firmly once filled.
- Lunch Boxes come in all shapes and sizes, ranging from metal to hard plastic and soft, thermo-insulated material. Many contain a vacuum bottle and a firm, unbreakable box for sandwiches.
  - Select a lunch box that has good insulation, or add insulation to your existing box by lining with firm polyurethane. Make sure there is a place in which the vacuum container fits securely. Should the box have other containers, check to see that the lids fit well and are also securely in place once they are inside the box.
  - For safety's sake, make sure the lunch box is waterproof and easily washed clean. Preheat or prechill the lunch containers as directed above. In very hot weather the box itself can be opened and chilled in the refrigerator overnight. Do not fill with food until just before leaving.
- Lunch Box Chillers. A special reusable plastic container filled with freezer gel can be placed in a lunch box to guarantee that food is kept absolutely cold. Chill or freeze the device overnight before adding to the box. Wash in warm, sudsy water, and rinse in cold

INTRODUCTION 11

water before chilling or freezing for reuse.
- Do-It-Yourself Lunch Containers. These range from a vacuum flask and plastic-bagged sandwich the executive packs into a briefcase to a can of juice and a piece of chicken a teenager stuffs into a tote bag. Here's what to use and what not to use:
  — *Plastic Containers* are especially made for portable lunches. They come in all shapes and sizes. While definitely not designed for keeping foods hot, they are ideal for packing every kind of portable cold food if placed within an insulated lunch box. They are light, nonbreakable, and easily cleaned; and they have excellent, tight-fitting lids. They are perfect for children's lunch boxes when safety is a prime consideration.
  — *Food Wraps* — plastic or aluminum, the choice is yours. Both have the advantage of adhering closely to the food to prevent drying out, and they are easily folded and sealed. They protect food well, in both refrigerator and freezer. However, for prolonged freezer-storage of foods, we recommend wrapping first in plastic, then adding an overwrap of foil. In every respect, although it is cheaper, we find wax paper to be less satisfactory. Freezer paper is an unnecessary luxury for food that is not planned for prolonged storage. Overwrapping food before placing it in a firm, insulated container keeps the container clean. Plastic or foil wrap alone must be considered insufficient protection for food.
  — *Plastic Bags* come in many different thicknesses and with many different closures. The most important usage tip is to press out all air from the bag before closing it with an air-tight seal. Thinner bags are best for refrigferator storage, thicker ones for freezer storage.

  Unlike plastic or foil wrap, plastic bags are reusable at least once or twice. Wash inside and out in warm, sudsy water, rinse in warm water, and hang to dry. Discard the bag should it contain the smallest hole or the seal be imperfect.

  Plastic-bagged food must be placed in a firm, insulated container for maximum food safety.
  — *Other Containers*. Many prepared foods come packed in reusable plastic containers. Budget-wise consumers will consider using them to supplement their lunch box equipment—a very smart step. But save them only if the lids seal tightly to the main container and they do not contain an odor from stongly seasoned foods.

Because of the possibility of breakage, it is not recommended that glass containers be reused, especially in children's lunch boxes.

FOOD SAFETY AND THE BROWN BAG LUNCH:

Cleanliness in handling and storing food is important at all times—but is assumes *real* importance when preparing portable lunches. Opportunities for food spoilage are so much more possible. Some traditional lunch foods tend to be spoilage prone; spoilage elements can creep in during preparation; an unhygenic environment created during storage, packing, and carrying can all add to food spoilage hazards. Being an alarmist is no help. Being aware of a few simple food safety rules is the best solution.

- *When Buying Food,* choose a supermarket that is clean; select food packaged in undamaged containers; notice the cleanliness of the personnel who handle the food—particularly in the meat, dairy, and delicatessen sections where cleanliness and freshness are especially important; select the freshest food possible, paying attention to "open dating" where necessary.
- *When Storing Food,* drive straight home from the market so foods do not become warm and begin to spoil. This is particularly important for foods from the refrigerator and freezer case. Store all canned and dried goods in a cool dry place. Make sure refrigerators and freezers are clean and the containers and overwraps used to protect food during storage are clean. Pay attention to storage dates and times. Check all foods frequently for signs of poor storage, remembering that dairy and meat products are especially vulnerable, particularly during summer months.
- *When Preparing Food,* make sure that hands, work surfaces, and utensils are clean, and that hot foods are really hot. This means bringing food to the boiling point (212°F) before packing *immediately*. Make sure cold foods are really cold. This means chilling as long as possible before packing *immediately* in insulated containers. Clean and chill all salad vegetables thoroughly.
- *When Packing Food,* make sure that all containers are scrupulously clean. Make sure, also, that your hands are clean before you wrap food. Check to see that insulated containers really work. Food that is held at "lukewarm" temperatures spoils most quickly. Preheat or prechill containers before using them.
- *While at School or on the Job,* remember not to store your lunch (even if in a well-insulated container) next to a radiator or in direct sunlight. If you have access to an office refrigerator, use it to store your lunch, particularly during the summer months. If food has been away from home longer than six hours and is neither very hot nor very cold, don't eat it. Point out the hazards to children of "trading" lunches. Everyone should be aware of the dangers involved in finishing a half-eaten snack at the end of the day.
- *Food-Safety Points on Returning Home.* Unpack the lunch box as

soon as possible on its return. Do not reuse plastic or foil wrap that has been in direct contact with food. Throw out any food remaining from lunch time. Wash out all containers, and clean the lunch box. Let all containers stand open as long as possible. Prechill containers for cold foods overnight, particularly during the summer months.
- *Super Food-Safety Points.* Meat, fish, egg, and dairy-based dishes are prone to quick spoilage. Fresh vegetables, fruits, and baked goods are not so vulnerable.

All foods must be prepared with care, but especially the ones mentioned above as being so perishable. Store them correctly; and above all, discard uneaten portions when they are brought home.

Discard immediately any food you suspect as being less than fresh.

1
SAVORY SOUPS AND SATISFYING STEWS

Two of the long-time staples of the lunch box, soups and stews, are easily and quickly made. Favorite vegetables and meats with a good fillip of seasoning are an instant "meal-in-a-dish" or "meal-in-a-thermos container" for many people, especially during fall and winter months.

Soups are easily homemade with the aid of a blender or food processor. And stews can be quickly simmered tender in less than twenty minutes if the right ingredients are selected.

NUTRITION KNOW-HOW:
- Select vegetables that contain good supplies of vitamins A and C.
- Preferred meats are chicken and turkey. Fish soups and stews are exotic for most people's lunch boxes. But the nutritionally astute gourmet in your family may be adventurous.
- Beef and pork (also lamb) should be trimmed free of fat before using.
- Veal, while nutritionally desirable (since it contains no fat), is an expensive luxury. If you wish, use in any of the chicken or turkey dishes.
- Use low-salt broths and bouillons as a base for soups and stews. Do not use supersalty bouillon cubes.
- Use minimum salt in the dish to taste. Better yet, substitute freshly grated lemon rind for salt. One teaspoon of grated lemon rind equals one teaspoon of salt. Lemon juice can also be used.
- Other salt substitutes are chopped fresh herbs—parsley with its added vitamin A advantage, dill, the chopped green part of scallions or chives, and chopped celery leaves.
- For complete nutrition, if the soup or stew does not contain pasta, rice, or potatoes, include a serving of whole-grain bread or crackers on the side.

SUPER-SPEEDY SOUPS AND STEWS:
- During the weekend when time is a little more available, prepare a batch or two of soup and stew. Divide into individual plastic con-

- tainers, label, and freeze. Thaw overnight in the refrigerator as needed, heating to the boiling point before you pour it into a prepared thermos container.
- A quick blend of low-sodium packed vegetables and cooked delicatessen meats, as soup or stew, with a big tablespoon of fresh herbs stirred in, makes a quick lunch box meal.
- For a real emergency, there is occasionally nothing wrong with a good quality canned soup or stew, but stir in a good measure of chopped parsley. And make sure low-salt crackers and a piece of fresh fruit are included in the lunch box.
- Crisp, store-bought crackers are good accompaniments to soups and stews. But make sure they are whole-grain and low-salt.

Consumer Notes On Soups and Stews

All soups should be quickly prepared, use low-salt seasonings, and minimize saturated fat ingredients. Nutrition and flavor should be high, cooking time and nonnutritional ingredients low.

Soups and stews should be heated to the boiling point (except where noted) before they are poured into a vacuum container.

Pack safely by heating the container with near-boiling water; let stand five minutes; drain. Pour one portion of the soup or stew into a container. Cook the remaining soup or stew; divide it between three individual freezer containers. Freeze until needed. These additional portions can be used later in lunch boxes by thawing them overnight and then heating, as above, before placing them in prepared vacuum containers.

All recipes are for four portions and can be easily divided or multiplied according to your needs.

BEEF VEGETABLE SOUP

2 tablespoons margarine or vegetable oil
½ cup chopped onion
½ cup thinly sliced celery
½ cup julienne strips carrots
½ cup thinly sliced mushrooms
½ cup fresh or frozen peas
1½ cups beef broth
½ cup water
2 tablespoons lemon juice
¼ cup chopped parsley
¼ to ½ teaspoon black pepper

1. In medium saucepan over low heat, melt margarine or heat oil. Add onion, celery, and carrots. Sauté, covered, until tender, about 5 to 7 minutes, stirring occasionally. Add mushrooms and peas, cook 2 minutes longer, stirring constantly.

SAVORY SOUPS AND SATISFYING STEWS 17

2. Stir in beef broth, water, and lemon juice. Simmer, covered, for 10 minutes. Stir in parsley and black pepper to taste. Pack the boiling-hot soup as directed at the beginning of this section. Makes four (approx. 1-cup) servings.

BLACK BEAN SOUP

2 tablespoons margarine or vegetable oil
½ cup finely chopped onion
1 large clove garlic, crushed
1 (10½-ounce) can black bean soup
1½ cups beef broth
2 to 4 tablespoons lemon juice
2 hard cooked eggs, coarsely chopped (optional)
¼ cup chopped parsley

1. In a medium saucepan, over low heat, melt the margarine or heat the oil. Add onion and garlic. Sauté, uncovered, until just tender, about 3 minutes, stirring constantly.
2. Add the black bean soup to the saucepan, together with the beef broth. Stir until smooth, beating with a whisk, if necessary.
3. Heat, covered, 5 minutes. Stir in lemon juice to taste. If desired, stir in coarsely chopped eggs; cook just to heat through. Do not boil. Stir in parsley. Pack the hot (not boiling) soup as directed at the beginning of this section. Makes four (¾-cup) servings.

Note: When preparing the remaining portions, thaw and reheat until piping hot. Do not boil; otherwise the eggs will toughen.

Nutrition Note: For a truly homemade soup with lower salt content, cook 1 (16-ounce) package dried black beans according to the label directions. Cook beans to a puree as directed, use 1½ cups purée in soup, freeze the remainder for later use. Omit eggs if you are concerned about cholesterol.

BORSCHT

2 tablespoons margarine or vegetable oil
1 cup chopped onion
1 large clove garlic, crushed
1 (16-ounce) can diced beets
1 (13¾-ounce) can beef broth
1 cup finely shredded cabbage
1 to 2 tablespoons cider vinegar

1. In a medium saucepan, over low heat, melt the margarine or heat

the oil. Add onion and garlic. Sauté, covered, until tender, about 5 minutes, stirring constantly.
2. Stir in the beets, beef broth, and cabbage. Simmer, covered, 10 minutes or until the cabbage is very tender. Add cider vinegar to taste. Pack the boiling-hot soup as directed at the beginning of this section. Makes four (approx. 1-cup) servings.

CHINESE SOUP

2 (13¾-ounce) cans chicken broth
2 to 4 tablespoons cider vinegar
1 to 2 tablespoons honey
2 eggs, beaten
½ cup finely shredded spinach
¼ cup finely sliced celery or water chestnuts
¼ cup bean sprouts
2 tablespoons thin radish slices

1. In a medium saucepan combine the chicken broth, cider vinegar, and honey. Bring to a boiling point, stirring to dissolve the honey.
2. While the mixture is boiling, slowly dribble in the beaten eggs to form small strings. Stir in the spinach, celery, bean sprouts, and radish slices. Heat 2 minutes. Do not boil. Pack the hot (not boiling) soup as directed at the beginning of this section. Makes four (approx. 1-cup) servings.

Note: When preparing the remaining portions, thaw and reheat only until piping hot. Do not boil; otherwise the eggs will toughen.

Nutrition Note: Traditionally 1 tablespoon soy sauce is added to this recipe, which would increase the salt content. Add only if desired, and use no more than 1 teaspoon. Cider vinegar and honey are added to taste, depending on the degree of sweet-sour flavor desired. Again, if you are concerned about cholesterol, omit the eggs.

CREAMY CORN CHOWDER

2 cups fresh-cut kernel corn, from 2 ears corn or 2 cups frozen kernel corn, from 1 (16-ounce) polybag
1 (13¾-ounce) can chicken broth
1 cup chopped celery with leaves
¼ teaspoon hot pepper sauce
¼ teaspoon nutmeg
½ teaspoon black pepper
1 cup light cream or whole milk

1. In a medium saucepan, combine 1 cup kernel corn with the chicken broth. Simmer, covered, 5 minutes until the corn is tender. Purée in a food processor or blender.
2. Return the creamed corn to the saucepan together with the remaining cup of kernel corn, celery with leaves, hot pepper sauce, nutmeg, and pepper. Simmer, covered, 5 minutes longer. Stir in the light cream or milk. Heat to the simmering point. Pack hot, not boiling, soup as directed as the beginning of this section. Makes four (approx. 1-cup) servings.

Nutrition Note: For a low-fat substitute for cream or milk, beat 1 (8-ounce) carton of unflavored, low-fat yogurt into the soup. Once the soup contains the yogurt, heat but do not boil; otherwise the mixture will curdle.

COUNTRY-STYLE POTATO SOUP

3 tablespoons margarine or vegetable oil
1 cup chopped onion
½ cup chopped celery
2 cloves garlic, crushed
1 cup diced, raw potato (¼-inch dice)
1 teaspoon grated lemon rind
¼ teaspoon black pepper
1 (13¾-ounce) can chicken broth
½ cup milk
¼ cup light or low-fat, unflavored yogurt
2 tablespoons chopped chives or scallions

1. In a medium saucepan, over low heat, melt the margarine or heat the oil. Add the onion, celery and garlic. Sauté, uncovered, 3 minutes, stirring constantly.
2. Add the potato, lemon rind, and pepper. Sauté 2 minutes longer. Stir in the chicken broth and milk. Simmer, covered, 10 to 15 minutes, or until the potato cubes are very tender. Beat in the light cream or low-fat yogurt and chives. Pack the hot (not boiling) soup as directed at the beginning of this section. Makes four (approx. 1-cup) servings.

Note: For the sophisticated brown bagger during the hot summer months, this soup makes a delicious cold addition to the lunch box. Purée the soup, while hot, in a food processor or blender. Chill, adding 2 to 4 tablespoons lemon juice for flavor. Freeze the surplus soup as directed.

FRESH TOMATO SOUP

2 tablespoons margarine or vegetable oil
½ cup finely chopped onion
1 clove garlic, crushed
2 cups chopped, peeled tomatoes
1 teaspoon grated lemon rind

1 (13¾-ounce) can beef broth
2 tablespoons lemon juice
¼ cup chopped dill
½ cup heavy or light cream (optional)

1. In a medium saucepan, over low heat, melt the margarine or heat the oil. Add the onions and garlic; sauté, uncovered, until just tender, about 3 to 5 minutes, stirring constantly.
2. Add the tomatoes and lemon rind. Sauté 3 minutes, stirring constantly. Add the beef broth, simmer, covered, 10 minutes, to blend the flavors. Stir in the lemon juice and dill. If desired, stir in the cream after cooking the soup 2 to 3 minutes. Pack the hot (not boiling) soup as directed at the beginning of this section. Makes four (approx. ¾-cup) servings.

Note: Once the cream is added, do not boil this soup. It will curdle.

Nutrition Note: For a low-fat soup, substitute unflavored low-fat yogurt for the heavy cream and omit lemon rind and lemon juice.

HONEST-TO-GOODNESS HEARTY VEGETABLE SOUP

3 tablespoons margarine or vegetable oil
½ cup chopped onion
2 cloves garlic, crushed
½ cup finely diced sweet potatoes
½ cup finely diced carrots
½ cup finely diced green peppers

½ cup tiny sprigs broccoli
1½ cups chicken broth
1 large tomato, peeled, seeded and diced
½ cup finely shredded spinach
½ teaspoon hot pepper sauce
2 to 3 tablespoons lemon juice

1. In a medium saucepan, over low heat, melt the margarine or heat the oil. Add the onion and garlic; sauté, uncovered, for 3 minutes, stirring constantly.
2. Add the sweet potatoes, carrots, green peppers, and broccoli sprigs. Sauté for 2 minutes, stirring constantly; stir in the chicken

broth. Simmer, covered, 10 to 15 minutes, or until the vegetables are just tender.
3. Stir in the tomatoes, spinach, and hot pepper sauce. Heat 2 minutes more just to cook the spinach. Stir in lemon juice to taste. Pack the boiling-hot soup as directed at the beginning of this section. Makes four (approx. 1½-cup) servings.

TURKEY NOODLE SOUP

2 tablespoons butter or margarine
1 cup chopped scallions or onions
1 cup finely chopped celery with leaves
½ cup finely diced carrots
1½ cups diced, cooked turkey meat (½-inch dice)
1½ cups chicken broth
6 strands spaghetti, broken into 1-inch pieces (about ½ cup)
½ teaspoon black pepper
¼ cup chopped parsley

1. In a medium saucepan, over low heat, melt the margarine or butter. Add the scallions, celery and carrots. Sauté, uncovered, 5 minutes, stirring constantly.
2. Stir in the diced, cooked turkey meat and chicken broth. Simmer, covered, 5 to 7 minutes, or until the vegetables are just tender.
3. Add spaghetti and pepper to saucepan; simmer, covered, 4 to 5 minutes, or until the spaghetti is "al dente"—that is, tender but still firm. Stir in the parsley. Pack the boiling-hot soup as directed at the beginning of this section. Makes four (approx. 1-cup) servings.

LEEK AND CHICKEN SOUP

2 tablespoons margarine or vegetable oil
1 cup thinly sliced leek
½ cup finely chopped onion
½ cup finely chopped celery
1 chicken breast half, bone and skin removed
1 teaspoon grated lemon rind
¼ teaspoon crushed thyme leaves
1½ cups chicken broth
½ cup water
¼ cup chopped celery leaves

1. In a medium saucepan, over low heat, melt the margarine or heat the oil. Add the leek, onion, and celery. Sauté, uncovered, until

tender, about 3 to 5 minutes, stirring constantly.
2. Cut the chicken into thin julienne strips. Add to the saucepan together with lemon rind and thyme leaves. Cook 2 to 3 minutes longer, stirring constantly.
3. Add the chicken broth and water. Simmer, covered, 10 minutes or until the chicken is tender. Stir in the celery leaves. Pack the boiling-hot soup as directed at the beginning of this section. Makes four (approx. ¾-cup) servings.

COUNTRY CAPTAIN STEW

2 small whole chicken breasts, bones removed
¼ cup flour
1 tablespoon paprika
¼ teaspoon black pepper
¼ cup vegetable oil
1 cup chopped onion
1 cup chopped green peppers
1 large clove garlic, crushed
1½ teaspoons curry powder
½ teaspoon ground mace or nutmeg
1 (16-ounce) can Italian plum tomatoes
½ cup dark raisins or currants
½ cup slivered almonds (optional)
¼ cup chopped parsley

1. Cut the chicken into ¾-inch cubes. Place the flour, paprika, and pepper in a clean paper or plastic bag; add the chicken cubes, and shake the contents to coat well. Reserve the surplus flour.
2. In a medium skillet, over medium heat, heat the oil. Brown the chicken cubes, cooking half at a time, turning frequently. As the chicken browns, remove it from the skillet, using a slotted spoon.
3. Add the onion, green pepper, and garlic to the skillet. Reduce the heat to low and cook the mixture 10 minutes, stirring occasionally. Add curry and mace; cook 2 minutes longer.
4. Stir in the tomatoes, breaking them up into small pieces with a spoon. Add the chicken; simmer, covered, 20 to 25 minutes, or until the chicken is tender. Stir in the raisins, almonds if desired, and parsley. Simmer 3 minutes longer. Pack the boiling-hot stew as directed at the beginning of this section. Makes four (approx. 1½-cup) servings.

Note: If the stew is too thin for your particular taste, blend 1 tablespoon of the reserved flour mixture with ¼ cup cold water; stir rapidly into the stew and bring it to the boiling point, stirring constantly.

SAVORY SOUPS AND SATISFYING STEWS

CHILI-TO-GO

1 pound ground beef
1 cup chopped onion
½ cup chopped celery
1 large clove garlic
1 to 3 teaspoons chili powder, depending on taste
1 (16-ounce) can Italian plum tomatoes
1 (16-ounce) can red kidney beans, rinsed and drained
1 to 2 tablespoons red wine vinegar
6 to 8 drops hot pepper sauce
¼ cup chopped celery leaves

1. In a medium skillet, over high heat, cook the beef, stirring it to break it into small pieces. As soon as the meat juices and fat appear in the skillet, add the onion, celery, and garlic.
2. Cook, stirring constantly, until the meat is brown. Drain off any surplus fat. Sprinkle chili powder, to taste, over the meat; cook 1 minute more, stirring well.
3. Stir in the tomatoes, breaking them into pieces with a spoon. Add the beans, mixing well. Bring to the boiling point; reduce the heat and gently simmer the tomatoes, covered, stirring them from time to time. Cook at least 30 minutes to develop the flavor.
4. Add vinegar and hot pepper sauce to taste; stir in the celery leaves. Pack the boiling-hot chili as directed at the beginning of this section. Makes four (approx. 1-cup) servings.

Nutrition Note: For the truly nutrition conscious who avoid the saturated fat of ground beef, raw ground turkey meat may be substituted (available at most major supermarkets). However, use 3 to 4 tablespoons of margarine or vegetable oil for browning the meat and raw vegetables.

NEW ENGLAND CHOWDER

2 tablespoons margarine
1 cup coarsely chopped onion
1 cup coarsely chopped celery, preferably the white part of the stalk
2 cups diced, fresh potatoes (⅓-inch dice)
3 cups milk
½ teaspoon black pepper
6 to 8 drops hot pepper sauce
1 pound fish fillets or fish steak, preferably flounder, white fish fillets, cod, or halibut steak
½ cup chopped celery leaves
1 tablespoon paprika

1. In medium saucepan, over low heat, melt the margarine. Add onions and celery; cook gently in a covered skillet for 10 minutes, stirring occasionally and being careful not to color or brown the vegetables.
2. Stir in the potatoes, coating them well with pan juices. Cook gently 2 minutes. Stir in the milk, pepper, and hot pepper sauce. Simmer, covered, 15 to 20 minutes or until the potatoes are tender.
3. Wipe the fish with damp paper towels; cut into ¾-inch cubes. Place the cubes on top of the potatoes and simmer, covered, until just tender, about 5 minutes. Sprinkle the celery leaves and paprika over the fish. Stir the chowder gently just to incorporate the fish and additional seasonings. Pack the hot (not boiling) chowder as directed at the beginning of this section. Makes four (approx. 1½-cup) servings.

Nutrition Note: Traditionally, clams are added to New England chowder. They are, however, high in salt. If desired, add 1 (7½-ounce) can clams and their liquor to the chowder with the white fish and reduce the milk to 2 cups. Also, for a lower fat content, use skim milk or nonfat, dry milk, reconstituted.

SAUSAGE AND PEPPERS

1 pound hot or sweet Italian sausages
1 cup julienne strips green peppers
1 cup julienne strips sweet red peppers
1 cup finely chopped onion
1 large clove garlic, crushed

2 tablespoons flour
1 (13¾-ounce) can chicken broth
1 to 3 teaspoons prepared Dijon-style mustard
¼ teaspoon black pepper
¼ cup chopped parsley

1. Prick the sausage skins thoroughly with a sharp-tined fork. In a medium skillet, over high heat, brown the sausages, turning them constantly. Reduce the heat as fat begins to appear in the skillet; do not brown the sausages too quickly. Allow 10 minutes for browning and partial cooking.
2. Remove the sausages from the skillet and drain them on paper towels. Add the green and red peppers to the fat remaining in the skillet; cook 5 minutes over a medium heat, stirring constantly. Remove the peppers from the skillet.
3. To the fat remaining in the skillet, add the onion and garlic; cook

for 5 minutes, stirring occasionally or until the onions are golden. Stir in the flour; cook 1 minute. Blend in the chicken broth, keeping the mixture smooth.
4. Cut the sausages into 1-inch pieces, and add them to the skillet together with the peppers. Stir in mustard and black pepper to taste. Simmer, covered, for 20 minutes. Stir in the chopped parsley. Pack the boiling-hot stew as directed at the beginning of this section. Makes four (approx. 1-cup) servings.

Nutrition Note: Pork and beef sausages or frankfurters have saturated fat and, though permissible occasionally, they certainly should not be a staple in anyone's diet. Chicken frankfurters can be found in some supermarkets. Substitute them for Italian sausages, and use 3 to 4 tablespoons of margarine or vegetable oil for browning. Chicken frankfurters have a low seasoning level; you may wish to increase the seasoning levels used. Kids would love beef franks in this recipe.

SWEET-SOUR TURKEY BARBECUE

2 tablespoons vegetable oil
1 cup finely chopped onions
2 large cloves garlic, crushed
2 tablespoons flour
1 teaspoon finely chopped fresh ginger root, or ¾ teaspoon powdered ginger
½ teaspoon crushed hot red pepper
1 (16-ounce) can crushed pineapple in natural juices
1 cup chopped, peeled tomato (1 large tomato)
2 tablespoons honey
2 tablespoons red wine vinegar
1 to 2 tablespoons prepared Dijon-style mustard
2 cups diced, cooked turkey meat, chicken, or lean pork (½-inch dice)

1. In a medium skillet, over medium heat, heat the oil. Add the onion and garlic, and cook for 5 minutes, stirring occasionally. Sprinkle the flour, ginger, and pepper over the mixture. Cook 1 minute more.
2. Drain the juice from the pineapple and blend the juice into the skillet; stir it until the mixture simmers. Add the crushed pineapple, tomato, honey, vinegar, and mustard to taste.
3. Stir in the diced turkey meat, chicken, or pork. Simmer, covered, for 10 minutes, stirring occasionally. Pack the boiling-hot stew as directed at the beginning of this section. Makes four (approx. 1-cup) servings.

TEXAS RED BEANS, RICE AND HAM

1 (16-ounce) can red kidney beans, rinsed and drained
1 cup chopped onion
1 large clove garlic, crushed
½ cup chopped scallions
1 cup chopped green peppers
½ cup chopped parsley
1 (16-ounce) can tomato puree
½ teaspoon black pepper
½ teaspoon hot pepper sauce
½ teaspoon crushed thyme leaves
½ teaspoon oregano
½ teaspoon cayenne pepper (optional)
½ cup long-grained rice
2 cups diced, precooked ham (½-inch dice)

1. In a medium saucepan combine the red beans, onions, garlic, scallions, pepper, and parsley. Stir in the tomato purée. Add black pepper, hot pepper sauce, thyme, oregano, and cayenne pepper, if desired.
2. Simmer, covered, over a low heat for 30 to 40 minutes or until the beans are very tender and the mixture very thick. Stir it occasionally to prevent sticking to the bottom of the pan.
3. Meanwhile, cook the rice according to the package label directions. Stir it into the bean mixture, together with the diced ham. Heat for 5 minutes. Pack the boiling-hot stew as directed at the beginning of this section. Makes four (approx. 1½-cup) servings.

Nutrition Note: You may substitute cooked diced turkey for the ham.

SPAGHETTI AND MEATBALLS

1 pound ground beef
½ cup fresh bread crumbs
¼ cup chopped parsley
1½ teaspoons dried basil
1½ teaspoons dried oregano
1 large clove garlic, crushed
1 egg
¼ cup milk
¼ cup olive oil
½ cup finely chopped onion
3 tablespoons flour
2 cups unsalted tomato juice
½ (8-ounce) package enriched spaghetti

1. Combine the ground beef, bread crumbs, parsley, 1 teaspoon each basil and oregano, and crushed garlic. Beat together the egg and milk, and stir them into the meat mixture. Knead gently with your hands to combine them thoroughly.
2. Roll the mixture into 1-inch meatballs; you should have approximately 24. In a large skillet, over medium heat, heat the olive oil.

Fry the meatballs, 8 at a time, turning them to all sides to brown them evenly. Set the meatballs aside.
3. Add onions to the oil remaining in the skillet; cook them for 5 minutes, stirring constantly. Stir in the flour; cook 1 minute more. Blend in the tomato juice, keeping the mixture smooth. Bring the mixture to the boiling point, stirring constantly. Stir in the remaining ½ teaspoon each of basil and oregano.
4. Return the meatballs to the skillet. Reduce the heat to low. Simmer, covered, 20 minutes or until the meatballs are tender. Meanwhile, cook the spaghetti according to the package label directions until it is "al dente"—tender but still firm. Drain and stir the cooked spaghetti into the meatballs. Pack the boiling-hot spaghetti and meatballs as directed at the beginning of this section. Makes four servings, each containing 6 meatballs and ¾ cup spaghetti with tomato sauce.

Note: For easy packing and serving you may wish to break the spaghetti into 1-inch pieces before cooking.

Nutrition Note: You may wish to omit the salt called for in the package label directions when you cook spaghetti. If so, add 1 tablespoon of olive oil and 1 garlic clove (crushed) to the cooking water. You may substitute raw ground turkey meat for ground beef.

TURKEY BEAN STEW

2 tablespoons olive or vegetable oil
1 cup finely chopped onion
2 large cloves garlic, crushed
1 (16-ounce) can white navy beans, rinsed and drained
1 cup diced peeled tomato (1 large tomato)
1 teaspoon crushed thyme leaves
1 teaspoon grated orange rind
½ teaspoon crushed rosemary leaves
½ teaspoon black pepper
1 (13¾-ounce) can chicken broth
2 cups diced, cooked turkey meat (½-inch dice)
½ cup chopped parsley

1. In a medium saucepan, over medium heat, heat the olive oil. Add onion and garlic; cook, uncovered, 5 minutes, stirring constantly.
2. Stir in the beans, tomato, thyme, orange rind, rosemary and pep-

per. Add the chicken broth; simmer, covered, 10 minutes. Add turkey meat; simmer, uncovered, 15 minutes, or until the broth is reduced by half, stirring occasionally.
3. Stir in parsley. Pack the boiling-hot stew as directed at the beginning of this section. Makes four (approx. 1-cup) servings.

Note: This stew is full of turkey and beans with enough broth left to moisten. The seasoning level may seem high, but the beans are bland and will absorb the seasoning as they cook.

CHICKEN, APPLE AND CORN STEW

- 2 small chicken breasts, bone removed
- 3 tablespoons margarine or vegetable oil
- ¾ cup chopped onion
- 1 small clove garlic, crushed
- 2 tablespoons flour
- ½ teaspoon crushed thyme leaves
- ¼ teaspoon black pepper
- 1 (13¾-ounce) can chicken broth
- 1 cup fresh or frozen kernel corn
- 1 cup thin slices tart apple (1 medium apple)
- 1 tablespoon chopped scallion or chives

1. Wipe the chicken with damp paper towels. Cut it into ½-inch cubes. In a medium saucepan, over medium heat, heat the margarine or oil. Brown the chicken cubes, half at a time, turning them so they cook evenly and removing them when golden brown.
2. Add onion and garlic; cook 2 minutes, stirring constantly. Sprinkle over the flour, thyme leaves, and pepper. Cook 1 minute more, stirring constantly. Blend in the chicken broth, and bring the mixture to the boiling point, stirring to keep smooth.
3. Return the chicken to the saucepan; add the kernel corn. Simmer, covered, 10 to 15 minutes. Gently stir in the apple slices; simmer, covered, 5 minutes more or until the apples are just tender. Stir in the chopped scallion or chives. Pack the boiling-hot stew as directed at the beginning of this section. Makes four (approx. 1-cup) servings.

Note: An added flavor fillip can be given to this stew by sprinkling in ½ teaspoon caraway seeds together with the thyme leaves and pepper.

2
SANDWICHES, SANDWICHES, SANDWICHES

A good sandwich continues to be the brown baggers' favorite lunch. How easy . . . just two pieces of excellent bread and a great filling put together the night before, or even moments before you leave. And a sandwich is still one of the best solutions to the lunch box meal.

Wise buys at the supermarket make sandwich-making simple. Just select whole-grain breads, chicken and turkey meats (avoid traditional sandwich meats that have a high fat content), and a variety of fresh fruit and vegetable salad makings.

For lunch makers looking to add a homemade dimension, here are six special breads—all do-ahead and freezer-storable—and fourteen fabulous new sandwich fillings.

NUTRITION KNOW-HOW:
- The home-baked breads in this chapter use enriched flour, whole grains, and low-fat or unsaturated fat ingredients. As in the recipes for quick muffins and breads, the nutritional bonus from these homemade breads is an important addition of vitamin B, iron, and fiber to your lunch box.
- For people who really watch sodium (the key element in salt), yeast-raised breads can be made without salt. And since there is no need for baking powder or baking soda, these breads have a much lower sodium content than quick muffins and breads.
- The best sandwich fillings are always moist and finely divided for easy spreading and eating. Traditional sandwich fillings tend to be high in fat content; these fillings are much lower.
- All fourteen fillings have the nutritional benefits of fresh ingredients with good fiber content, vitamin A, B, and C. Add a further boost by layering finely shredded salad vegetables between the bread and the filling. Thin shreds of spinach, tomato slices, or grated carrot can be added to build multilayered sandwiches.

Consumer Notes on Breads and Fillings

Any baked good—but especially bread—needs extra care to ensure perfection. The end results, plus the cost of ingredients and time involved in making breads, make this a real necessity.

- Read the baking tips given at the beginning of the chapter on "Quick Muffins and Breads."
- In addition, remember:
  - Warm temperatures are the secret of good breadmaking. Cold and drafts will kill the yeast too soon, as will liquid or temperatures above 115°F—except the final high oven temperature, which is essential to stop the action of the yeast.
  - Correct consistency of the dough is important; it should be neither too dry nor too sticky.
  - Allow sufficient time for the dough to rise.
  - Make sure the oven temperature is correct and the bread is baked on a shelf set in the lower third of the oven.
  - Place two loaf pans side by side, not one above the other.
  - Once cooled completely and wrapped with an airtight wrapper, these breads will keep a week in the refrigerator and at least six months in the freezer. Label and date before freezing.
- For fillings, remember:
  - Divide finely so they can be eaten easily.
  - Fillings keep only forty-eight hours in the refrigerator. Fillings containing fresh fruits and vegetables, jams, jellies, cottage cheese, mayonnaise, and nuts do not freeze well.
  - Sandwich fillings made of sliced meats, firm cheeses, and prepared fish do freeze well.

Pack sandwiches safely by wrapping them in plastic wrap or aluminum foil and placing them in a box that cannot be crushed. All cold sandwiches should be placed in a cold, clean, insulated lunch box. Any sandwiches not eaten *must be* discarded.

THE NONSOGGY SANDWICH:

Sandwiches should be neither dry nor soggy. This is why sandwich bread is spread with butter, margarine, mayonnaise, or sour cream. Use very little even if you decide to add fat to your lunch box this way. Use margarine to avoid the saturated fats of dairy products; use low-fat spreadable cheeses as an alternate. Or use low-calorie, fat-reduced versions of other sandwich spreads. Also see page 143 for alternate bread spreads in the Quick Nutrition "Fix-Its" chapter.

FARM HOUSE OATMEAL BREAD

1 cup old-fashioned rolled oats
1½ cups boiling water
¼ cup dark molasses
1 to 1½ teaspoons salt (optional)
1 cup milk or low-fat milk
2 envelopes dry active yeast
5 to 6 cups all-purpose flour

1. Place oats in large bowl; add boiling water, stirring well. Add molasses and salt, if desired, stirring well to dissolve. Let stand 5 minutes.
2. Heat milk just until "lukewarm," pour over yeast in a small bowl; stir well to dissolve. Stir into oat mixture.
3. Add all-purpose flour, 1 cup at a time, to oat mixture, stirring vigorously between each addition. Add sufficient flour to make a soft, nonsticky dough.
4. Turn dough onto lightly floured surface. Knead 10 minutes, adding additional flour to prevent dough from sticking. Place dough in clean, greased bowl, turning to grease all sides of dough.
5. Cover dough with damp towel; let rise in warm, draft-free place for 1 hour or until double in bulk.
6. Punch dough down; turn onto lightly floured surface. Knead 30 seconds. Divide dough in half, shape into 2 loaves. Place in 2 well-greased 9 × 5 × 3-inch loaf pans. Cover with damp towel; let rise in warm, draft-free place 1 hour or until double in bulk.
7. Bake in preheated 375°F oven for 45 to 50 minutes, or until loaves are brown and sound hollow when tapped on bottom. Remove from pans immediately to wire rack to cool. Makes two 9 × 5 × 3-inch loaves.

Note: This loaf uses a heavy grain and will require longer to rise than lighter loaves.
   Do not use quick-cooking oats in this bread.

OLD-FASHIONED WHITE BREAD

2½ cups milk or low-fat milk
¼ cup margarine
2 tablespoons honey or brown sugar
1 envelope dry active yeast
6 to 7 cups all-purpose enriched flour
1 to 1½ teaspoons salt (optional)

1. In medium saucepan combine milk, margarine (cut in small

pieces), and honey. Heat over low heat, stirring constantly, just to melt margarine and dissolve honey. Cool liquid, if necessary, to "lukewarm," i.e., a drop on your wrist will feel comfortable.
2. In large bowl combine yeast with 1 cup liquid. Stir well to dissolve; stir in remaining liquid.
3. Add all-purpose flour to yeast mixture, 1 cup at a time, stirring vigorously to keep mixture smooth and adding salt if desired along with flour. Add sufficient flour to make a soft, nonsticky dough.
4. Turn dough onto lightly floured surface, knead 10 minutes, adding additional flour to prevent dough from sticking. Place dough in clean, greased, large bowl, turning to grease all sides of dough.
5. Cover dough with damp towel; let rise in warm, draft-free place for 1 hour or until double in bulk.
6. Punch dough down; turn onto lightly floured surface. Knead 30 seconds. Divide dough in half and shape into 2 loaves. Place in 2 well-greased 9 × 5 × 3-inch loaf pans. Cover with damp towel; let rise in warm, draft-free place for 40 minutes or until double in bulk.
7. Bake in preheated 400°F oven for 40 to 45 minutes or until loaves are brown and sound hollow when tapped on bottom. Remove from pans immediately to wire rack to cool. Makes two 9 × 5 × 3-inch loaves.

Nutrition Note: As with all baked goods using all-purpose flour, make sure you use all-purpose, *enriched* flour.

POTATO DILLY BREAD

2½ cups milk or low-fat milk
⅓ cup sugar
⅓ cup margarine
1 envelope dry active yeast
1 cup fresh (not instant) mashed potatoes

2 to 3 tablespoons freshly snipped dill weed or 1 to 2 tablespoons dried dill
6 to 7 cups all-purpose flour

1. In medium saucepan combine milk, sugar, and margarine (cut into small pieces). Heat over low heat, stirring constantly just to dissolve sugar and melt margarine. Cool liquid, if necessary, to "lukewarm," i.e., a drop on your wrist will feel comfortable.
2. In large bowl, combine yeast with 1 cup milk. Stir well to dissolve. Add mashed potatoes, beating to a smooth batter. Then stir in remaining liquid and dill weed to taste.

SANDWICHES, SANDWICHES, SANDWICHES

3. Add all-purpose flour to yeast mixture, 1 cup at a time, stirring vigorously to keep mixture smooth. Add sufficient flour to make a soft, nonsticky dough.
4. Turn dough onto lightly floured surface. Knead 10 minutes, adding additional flour to prevent dough from sticking. Place dough in clean, greased, large bowl, turning to grease all sides of dough.
5. Cover dough with damp towel; let rise in warm, draft-free place for 1 hour or until double in bulk.
6. Punch dough down, turn onto lightly floured surface. Knead 30 seconds. Divide dough in half and shape into 2 loaves. Place in 2 well-greased 9 × 5 × 3-inch loaf pans. Cover with damp towel; let rise in warm, draft-free place for 45 to 60 minutes or until double in bulk.
7. Bake in preheated 375°F oven for 40 to 45 minutes or until loaves are brown and sound hollow when tapped on bottom. Remove from pans immediately to wire rack to cool. Makes two 9 × 5 × 3-inch loaves.

Nutrition Note: Dill weed is a wonderfully savory addition to bread and eliminates anyone's need for salt.

PUMPERNICKEL BREAD

2½ cups milk or low-fat milk
⅓ cup dark brown sugar firmly packed
¼ cup margarine
2 envelopes dry active yeast
1 tablespoon unsweetened cocoa powder
1 tablespoon freeze-dried coffee, crushed to fine powder
4 cups all-purpose flour
1½ cups dark rye flour
½ cup yellow cornmeal
1 to 1½ teaspoons salt (optional)

1. In medium saucepan combine milk, brown sugar, and margarine (cut into small pieces). Heat over low heat, stirring constantly, just to dissolve sugar and melt margarine. Cool liquid, if necessary, to "lukewarm," i.e., a drop on your wrist will feel comfortable.
2. In large bowl, combine yeast with 1½ cups liquid. Stir well to dissolve. Stir cocoa powder and coffee into 1 cup liquid remaining in saucepan; set aside.
3. In second large bowl, combine all-purpose flour, rye flour, yellow cornmeal, and salt, if desired. Add 1 cup flour mixture to yeast mixture, stirring vigoursly to keep dough smooth.
4. Add ½ cup cocoa-coffee liquid and 1 cup flour mixture. Stir

vigorously to keep dough smooth. Repeat, using last ½ cup cocoa-coffee liquid and 1 cup flour mixture. Continue to add flour mixture to make a soft, nonsticky dough.

5. Turn dough onto lightly floured surface. Knead 10 minutes, adding additional all-purpose flour to prevent dough from sticking. Place dough in clean, greased, large bowl, turning to grease all sides of dough.
6. Cover dough with damp towel; let rise in a warm, draft-free place for 1 hour or until double in bulk.
7. Punch dough down; turn onto lightly floured surface. Knead 30 seconds. Divide dough in half and shape into 2 loaves. Place into 2 well-greased 9 × 5 × 3-inch loaf pans. Cover with damp towel; let rise in warm, draft-free place for 45 minutes or until double in bulk.
8. Bake in preheated 375°F oven for 40 minutes or until loaves sound hollow when tapped on bottom. Remove from pans immediately to wire rack to cool. Makes two 9 × 5 × 3-inch loaves.

GRANARY BREAD

2½ cups milk or low-fat milk
⅓ cup margarine
¼ cup honey or molasses
2 packages dry active yeast
1 to 1½ teaspoons salt (optional)
2 to 3 cups all-purpose flour
2 cups whole wheat flour
1 cup rye flour
1 cup quick-cooking rolled oats

1. In medium saucepan combine milk, margarine (cut in small pieces), and honey. Heat over low heat, stirring constantly, just to melt margarine and dissolve honey. Cool liquid, if necessary, to "lukewarm," i.e., a drop on your wrist will feel comfortable.
2. In large bowl, combine yeast with 1 cup liquid. Stir well to dissolve; stir in remaining liquid, adding salt if desired.
3. In second large bowl, combine 2 cups all-purpose flour, whole wheat flour, rye flour, and rolled oats. Add, 1 cup at a time, to yeast mixture, stirring vigorously to keep mixture smooth. Add remaining 1 cup all-purpose flour, if necessary, to make a soft, nonsticky dough.
4. Turn dough onto lightly floured surface. Knead 10 minutes, adding additional all-purpose flour to prevent dough from sticking. Place dough in clean, greased, large bowl, turning to grease all sides of dough.
5. Cover dough with damp towel; let rise in warm, draft-free place

for 1 hour or until double in bulk.
6. Punch dough down, turn onto lightly floured surface. Knead 30 seconds. Divide dough in half and shape into 2 loaves. Place in 2 well-greased 9 × 5 × 3-inch loaf pans. Cover with damp towel; let rise in warm, draft-free place for 1 hour or until double in bulk.
7. Bake in preheated 375°F oven for 45 to 50 minutes or until loaves are brown and sound hollow when tapped on bottom. Remove from pans immediately to wire rack to cool. Makes two 9 × 5 × 3-inch loaves.

WHOLE-WHEAT BREAD

3 cups milk or low-fat milk
⅓ cup margarine
⅓ cup honey or brown sugar, firmly packed
2 envelopes dry active yeast
4 cups all-purpose flour
4 cups whole-wheat flour
1 to 1½ teaspoons salt (optional)

1. In medium saucepan, combine milk, margarine (cut in small pieces), and honey. Heat over low heat, stirring constantly, just to melt margarine and dissolve honey. Cool liquid, if necessary, to "lukewarm," i.e., a drop on your wrist should feel comfortable.
2. In large bowl, combine yeast with 1 cup liquid. Stir well to dissolve; stir in remaining liquid.
3. In second large bowl, mix together all-purpose flour and whole-wheat flour, adding salt if desired. Add flour mixture to yeast mixture, 1 cup at a time, stirring vigorously to keep mixture smooth. Add sufficient flour to make a soft, nonsticky dough.
4. Turn dough onto lightly floured surface. Knead 10 minutes, adding additional flour to prevent dough from sticking. Place dough in clean, greased, large bowl, turning to grease all sides of dough.
5. Cover dough with damp towel; let rise in a warm, draft-free place for 1 hour or until double in bulk.
6. Punch dough down, turn onto lightly floured surface. Knead 30 seconds. Divide dough in half and shape into 2 loaves. Place in 2 well-greased 9 × 5 × 3-inch loaf pans. Cover with damp towel; let rise in a warm, draft-free place for 40 minutes or until double in bulk.
7. Bake in preheated 375°F oven for 45 to 50 minutes or until loaves are brown and sound hollow when tapped on bottom. Remove from pans immediately to wire rack to cool. Makes two 9 × 5 × 3-inch loaves.

Nutrition Note: Some people say bread needs salt; not true, but given as an optional ingredient, here is the acceptable range you may want to add. Better yet, try substituting 1½ teaspoons grated lemon rind.

MEXICAN BEEF FILLING

½ pound ground beef
¼ cup chopped onion
1 small clove garlic, crushed
1 teaspoon chili powder
¼ teaspoon hot pepper sauce

1 8-ounce can tomato purée
1 8-ounce can red kidney beans, drained
1 tablespoon red wine vinegar

1. In medium skillet, over medium heat, cook beef, stirring to break into small pieces. Add onion and garlic; cook 5 to 7 minutes until beef is browned. Add chili powder and hot pepper sauce.
2. Stir in tomato purée, drained beans, and vinegar. Simmer, uncovered, until mixture is very thick, stirring to break up beans. Cook and chill to use as filling, layering onto sandwiches with shredded lettuce and sliced tomatoes. Makes 2½ cups filling, enough for two to three generous sandwiches.

Nutrition Note: Ground raw turkey may be used instead of ground beef. However, add 2 tablespoons vegetable oil in order to brown turkey and vegetables.

AVOCADO SALAD FILLING

1 small ripe avocado
⅓ to ½ cup low-fat, unflavored yogurt
2 tablespoons lemon juice
1 teaspoon grated lemon rind
¼ teaspoon hot pepper sauce, or to taste

½ cup peeled, diced tomatoes, seeds removed (1 large tomato)
½ cup grated zucchini
2 tablespoons grated onion

1. Peel avocado; remove pit and cut into chunks. Place in blender or food processor container; add low-fat, unflavored yogurt (quantity depending on ripeness of avocado), lemon juice, lemon rind and hot pepper sauce. Blend or process until of purée consistency.
2. Gently fold in diced tomatoes (draining off any liquid), grated

zucchini, and onion. Makes 2 cups filling; enough for two to three sandwiches.

Note: Avocado salad filling can be made ahead overnight and stored in a plastic refrigerator container. Press plastic wrap directly onto the surface of the filling before snapping the lid in place. This will prevent the filling from discoloring.

CHEESE AND CHUTNEY FILLING

1 cup finely shredded sharp Cheddar cheese (about 4 ounces)
½ cup chopped tart apple
½ cup finely shredded Iceberg lettuce

2 tablespoons finely chopped or grated onion
½ cup Indian-style chutney or sweet corn relish

In medium bowl combine grated cheese, chopped apple, lettuce, and onion. Stir in chutney or relish to moisten dry ingredients. If chutney contains large pieces of vegetable and fruit, drain liquid into dry ingredients, chop solids finely, and add to filling. Makes 1½ cups filling, enough for two sandwiches.

Note: The sharpness of the cheese used can vary according to taste.

Nutrition Note: A skim-milk cheese may be substituted for Cheddar cheese.

CHICKEN LIVER AND MUSHROOM FILLING

2 tablespoons vegetable oil or margarine
½ pound chicken livers, trimmed and cut in half
½ pound fresh mushrooms, trimmed and wiped clean

3 to 4 tablespoons mayonnaise or low-fat, unflavored yogurt
½ cup chopped parsley
½ teaspoon black pepper

1. In medium skillet over medium heat, cook chicken livers until tender but just pink in center, stirring constantly, about 5 minutes. Remove with slotted spoon to container of food processor.
2. In remaining pan drippings, cook mushrooms until tender, stirring constantly, about 3 to 4 minutes. Add mushrooms and pan

drippings to food processor. Process only until smooth.
3. In bowl, mix chicken liver mixture with sufficient mayonnaise or low-fat yogurt to make spreadable. Stir in parsley and pepper. Makes 1¾ cups filling, enough for two generous sandwiches.

Nutrition Note: Even chicken livers are a sometime treat.

DELI EGG SALAD FILLING

4 hard-cooked eggs, finely chopped
½ cup diced roasted sweet red peppers from 1 7-ounce jar
⅓ cup finely chopped radishes
2 tablespoons finely chopped or grated onions
3 to 4 tablespoons mayonnaise or low-fat unflavored yogurt
1 tablespoon prepared Dijon-style mustard
4 to 6 drops hot pepper sauce

In medium bowl combine chopped hard-cooked eggs, red peppers, radishes, and onion. Add sufficient mayonnaise or yogurt just to moisten. Stir in prepared mustard and hot pepper sauce to taste. Makes 1¼ cups filling, enough for two sandwiches.

Nutrition Note: Again, this is a salad filling traditionally using mayonnaise; low-fat unflavored yogurt is a better nutritional alternate. Eggs are a sometime treat in your lunch box. They have a high cholesterol content.

CHICKEN WALDORF FILLING

1 cup finely diced, cooked chicken (about 4 ounces)
½ cup finely chopped, unpeeled red apple
¼ cup finely chopped celery
¼ cup chopped walnuts
½ teaspoon celery seed
¼ teaspoon black pepper
3 to 4 tablespoons mayonnaise or low-fat, unflavored yogurt

In medium bowl combine diced cooked chicken, chopped apple, celery, and walnuts. Stir in celery seed and pepper. Add sufficient mayonnaise or unflavored yogurt to moisten. Makes 1¾ cups filling, enough for two sandwiches.

SANDWICHES, SANDWICHES, SANDWICHES

Nutrition Note: While it is traditional to use mayonnaise for this salad filling, low-fat unflavored yogurt will have fewer calories and less fat—though a sharper flavor.

SEAFOOD SALAD

- 1 8-ounce can salmon, crabmeat or tiny shrimp, drained
- ½ cup low-fat, small curd cottage cheese
- ½ cup grated zucchini
- ½ cup grated radishes
- 1 tablespoon snipped chives or green onions
- 1 tablespoon lemon juice
- ½ teaspoon grated lemon rind
- ¼ teaspoon black pepper

In medium bowl flake seafood, if necessary, removing any skin and cartilege. Gently stir in cottage cheese, grated zucchini, radishes, snipped chives, lemon juice, lemon rind, and pepper. Makes 1½ cups filling, enough for two sandwiches.

Nutrition Note: Convenience seafoods such as the ones in this recipe should be an occasional treat only, since they contain high levels of fat and cholesterol. The truly nutritionally aware brown bagger will substitute 1 cup cooked and flaked whitefish—cod, flounder, sole.

TUNA SALAD FILLING

- 1 7½-ounce can water-packed tuna, drained and flaked
- ¼ cup finely chopped celery
- ¼ cup finely chopped onion
- ¼ cup finely chopped green or sweet red peppers
- 1 tablespoon lemon juice
- 1 teaspoon grated lemon rind
- 3 to 4 tablespoons low-fat, unflavored yogurt or mayonnaise

In medium bowl flake tuna; add chopped celery, onion, and pepper. Stir in lemon juice and lemon rind. Add sufficient unflavored yogurt or mayonnaise just to moisten. Makes 1½ cups filling, enough for two sandwiches.

Nutrition Note: Water-packed tuna lowers the calories and fat content of this filling, as does using low-fat, unflavored yogurt. Lemon as a seasoning is a good alternate to salt.

BARBECUE FRANKS FILLING

4 beef frankfurters
½ cup chopped onion
½ cup chopped green peppers
1 to 2 teaspoons chili powder
2 tablespoons tomato paste

2 tablespoons brown sugar
1 tablespoon cider vinegar
½ cup water or low-salt beef broth

1. In medium skillet, over medium heat, fry frankfurters on all sides until brown and cooked thoroughly, about 7 to 10 minutes. Remove from skillet; cool and dice finely.
2. In fat remaining in skillet (add 1 tablespoon vegetable oil if necessary), brown onion and green peppers. Stir in chili powder, tomato paste, brown sugar, mustard, and vinegar.
3. Add water or chicken broth and diced frankfurters. Simmer until very thick, stirring to prevent sticking. Cool and chill to use as filling. Makes 2 cups filling, enough for two generous sandwiches.

Nutrition Note: In many areas chicken and even turkey frankfurters are available as a substitute for beef frankfurters.

PEANUT BUTTER AND BACON FILLING

6 to 8 slices bacon, fried crisp and crumbled
½ cup creamy peanut butter
2 to 3 tablespoons milk or low-fat milk

½ cup finely grated carrot
¼ cup finely chopped celery
1 to 2 tablespoons grated onion
4 to 6 drops hot pepper sauce

In medium skillet fry bacon slices until crisp; drain on paper towels. Cool and crumble to measure ½ cup. In medium bowl beat peanut butter until soft, adding sufficient milk to make consistency of heavy cream. Stir in bacon, carrot, celery, onion, and hot pepper sauce. Makes 1½ cups filling, enough for two sandwiches.

HAM AND APPLE FILLING

1 cup ground cooked ham (about 4 ounces)
½ cup chopped celery
½ cup chopped toasted almonds

⅓ to ½ cup unsweetened applesauce
¼ teaspoon finely crumbled sage or poultry seasoning

In medium bowl combine ground ham (you may finely chop ham if more convenient), celery, and almonds. Stir in sufficient applesauce to make moist and spreadable. Season with sage. Makes 1¾ cups filling, sufficient for two sandwiches.

Nutrition Note: Chicken or turkey may be substituted for the ham; applesauce is a good low-calorie, low-fat moistening ingredient.

TURKEY PINEAPPLE FILLING

- 1 cup finely diced cooked turkey (about 4 ounces)
- 1 8-ounce can crushed pineapple in natural juices, well-drained
- ½ cup finely chopped green peppers
- ½ cup chopped unsalted dry roasted peanuts
- ¼ cup chopped dates
- 1 tablespoon lemon juice
- ½ teaspoon grated lemon rind
- 3 to 4 tablespoons mayonnaise or low-fat, unflavored yogurt

In medium bowl combine diced cooked turkey, crushed pineapple, green peppers, peanuts, and dates. Stir in lemon juice and lemon rind and sufficient mayonnaise or unflavored yogurt just to moisten. Makes 2 cups filling, enough for two generous sandwiches.

Nutrition Note: The bonus is turkey, no salt, and your choice of using low-fat, unflavored yogurt.

CHINESE VEGETABLE SALAD FILLING

- ½ cup mashed bean curd (tofu) — 1 2-ounce square tofu
- ⅓ to ½ cup milk or low-fat milk
- 1 teaspoon grated fresh ginger root or ¼ teaspoon powdered ginger
- 1 teaspoon grated orange rind
- 2 medium tomatoes, peeled, seeded and diced (about 1 cup, well drained)
- ½ cup chopped green pepper
- ½ cup chopped bamboo shoots
- ½ cup chopped water chestnuts
- ½ cup fresh bean sprouts

1. In medium bowl beat mashed bean curd with sufficient milk to make consistency of heavy cream; stir in ginger and orange rind.

2. Gently fold in diced tomatoes, chopped green peppers, bamboo shoots, water chestnuts, and bean sprouts. Makes 2½ cups filling; enough for two to three generous sandwiches.

COTTAGE CHEESE AND FRUIT FILLING

1 8-ounce container low-fat, large curd cottage cheese, drained
1 small orange, peeled, sectioned and chopped
½ cup chopped tart apple, unpeeled
1 8-ounce can crushed pineapple in natural juices, drained
1 teaspoon grated lemon rind
¼ to ½ teaspoon curry powder

In medium bowl combine cottage cheese, chopped fresh orange, apple, and drained pineapple. Stir in lemon rind and curry powder. Makes 2 cups filling, enough for two sandwiches.

3
SUPER SANDWICHES

What's better than a super-stuffed sandwich? It's the hero of every brown bag. Made of layer upon layer of savory cold meats and deliciously crisp vegetables, it's the mouth-watering lunch at the end of a long morning's work.

The super sandwich comes in many shapes and with many flavor combinations. Whether you call it a submarine, hogie, or grinder, it's a hero; then there's the New Orleans Poor Boy, filled pita bread, the double decker, the triple decker, stuffed club roll, french bread, or tortilla. There's even a super filling contained by lettuce leaves.

These sandwiches are super in every way. They are an occasional indulgence since they contain ingredients that have nutritional concerns as well as nutritional pluses. They are bigger-than-usual sandwiches. And they are a gourmet item in the lunch box. They require more time to fix and an appreciation that they are not two slices of bread with a familiar filling. But for a special person and a special midday meal, they are well worth the effort.

NUTRITION KNOW-HOW:
- When making multi-layered sandwiches, avoid the traditional processed and packaged sliced meats. Bolognas, salamis, and chopped pressed sandwich meats that are pre-sliced are high in saturated fats and salt. Sliced chicken and turkey are the super-nutritional staple of these sandwiches.
- Beef, ham, liver, eggs, and fatty fish such as salmon and herring have nutritional pluses and some nutritional minuses. They are excellent sources of protein, iron, and the vitamin B complex. Unfortunately, they are also sources of saturated fat and cholesterol.
- Eat these last-mentioned foods occasionally for their nutritional advantages, and be particularly sparing in your consumption of eggs and liver.
- Most of the breads in this chapter are store-bought. Try to find whole-wheat rolls to use as the basis of your super sandwiches. Or make your own.
- The attraction of super sandwiches is their exciting layers of meats

and salad vegetables. And the benefit of salad vegetables is their fiber and vitamin content.
- So super sandwiches are a main dish and a salad or vegetable dish all in one. All are a good nutritional midday boost.

Consumer Notes on Breads and Fillings.
- These sandwiches can be made ahead, wrapped tightly in foil or plastic wrap and chilled overnight. They will be crisp—but not super-crisp.
- You may prefer to prepare the sandwich makings ahead, pack them separately, and chill them overnight before placing them in the lunch box. A super-crisp sandwich is assured if your brown bagger assembles it on the spot.
- Many of these super sandwiches are secured by toothpicks. Make sure the toothpicks you use have multicolored cellophane ruffles at one end that will alert your luncher to remove them.
- *Pack food safely* by making sure all ingredients are fresh, especially sliced meats. Chill as soon as the sandwiches are made. Pack them in rigid containers to avoid crushing them. For transporting, carry them in an insulated lunch box. As with any lunch box food, any that is not eaten should be discarded.

CHICKEN LIVER FILLED FRENCH ROLL

1 individual crisp French roll (about 5 to 6 inches long)

Filling

2 tablespoons margarine	**Low-fat, unflavored yogurt**
¼ cup finely chopped onions	**Crumbled thyme leaves to**
¼ pound chicken livers,	**taste**
washed, trimmed and halved	**Black pepper to taste**

1. Cut end off French roll and reserve. Using long-handled iced-tea spoon, remove soft crumb from roll to leave a hollow "tube" with a crusty wall about ¼-inch thick. Reserve crumbs.
2. In medium skillet heat margarine. Cook onions over low heat 2 minutes. Add chicken livers. Cook 5 to 7 minutes until cooked through but still slightly pink at center.
3. In blender or food processor, process bread crumbs until fine. Remove and set aside. Process chicken livers, onions, and pan drippings until coarsely chopped.
4. Combine chicken livers and crumbs. Add a little yogurt if mixture

is dry. Season to taste with thyme and black pepper. Use mixture to fill hollow roll. Secure end of roll in place with toothpick. Makes one serving.

Nutrition Note: Chicken liver is an excellent and essential source of iron. Include only occasionally in your lunch box because of its cholesterol content.

CHICKEN PATÉ FILLED FRENCH ROLL

1 individual crisp French roll (about 5 to 6 inches long)

Filling

1 7-ounce can chunk-style chicken or 1 cup diced, cooked chicken	½ cup chopped mushrooms
	¼ cup chopped parsley
	Grated lemon rind, to taste
½ cup chopped pimiento-stuffed green olives	Black pepper, to taste
	Poultry seasoning, to taste

1. Prepare French roll as in previous recipe. Reserve crumbs.
2. Prepare filling by puréeing chunk-style chicken in blender or food processor. Stir in (do not process) olives, mushrooms, and parsley, plus lemon rind, black pepper, and poultry seasoning to taste.
3. If mixture is very moist, stir in bread crumbs until mixture has soft spreading consistency. Place filling in roll as in previous recipe. Secure roll end in position with toothpick. Makes one serving.

NEW ORLEANS POOR BOY SANDWICH

1 individual French roll (about 5 to 6 inches long	1 tablespoon margarine
	¼ teaspoon celery seed

Filling

1 7½-ounce can water-packed tuna, drained and flaked	1 to 2 tablespoons capers, drained, or 1 tablespoon prepared horseradish
¼ cup chopped celery	Low-fat, unflavored yogurt
¼ cup chopped parsley	Grated lemon rind to taste
	Black pepper to taste

1. Cut top from roll; reserve. Using a teaspoon, hollow out soft crumb from roll, leaving the crusty shell of the roll, about ¼-inch thick. Crumble crumbs to measure ½ cup.
2. Blend margarine and celery seed together. Spread over inside walls of roll and the cut surface of the top.
3. Make filling by blending flaked tuna, celery, parsley, and capers. Add ½ cup crumbs, and enough yogurt to bind and moisten the filling. Add lemon rind and black pepper to taste.
4. Place filling inside roll. Secure top in place with toothpicks. Makes one serving.

Note: The original New Orleans Poor Boy contained oysters, today an ingredient too rich for both the pocketbook and the diet. This tuna-fish version stretched with breadcrumbs is both budget and nutrition conscious.

NEW ORLEANS RICH BOY SANDWICH

1 individual French roll (about 5 to 6 inches long)
1 to 2 tablespoons margarine
1 tablespoon chopped parsley
Grated lemon rind to taste

Filling

¼ cup finely chopped mushrooms
4 ounces cooked bay scallops or flaked white fish (about ⅔ cup)
4 stalks cooked asparagus, cut in ½-inch diagonal pieces
Low-fat, unflavored yogurt
Grated lemon rind, to taste
Black pepper to taste

1. Prepare French roll as in previous recipe, spreading with a blend of margarine, parsley, and lemon rind to taste. Do not reserve crumbs.
2. Place chopped mushrooms as bottom layer in roll. Blend together scallops and asparagus (binding and moistening with a little yogurt) with grated lemon rind and black pepper to taste.
3. Place filling inside roll. Secure top in place with toothpicks. Makes one serving.

Note: The ingredients here are luxurious—something not to buy specially, but to use from a leftover dinner the night before—certainly a gourmet touch to a very adult lunch box.

B.L.T. DOUBLE DECKER SANDWICH

3 slices whole-wheat bread   1 to 2 tablespoons margarine

Filling

Boston Lettuce leaves, in bite size pieces
Tomato slices
Onion rings

4 to 6 bacon slices, very crisply fried
Black pepper to taste

1. Toast bread, if desired. Spread margarine on *one* side of two slices of bread and on *both* sides of third slice of bread.
2. Set one slice of bread spread side uppermost and top with half of lettuce pieces, tomato slices, onion rings, and two to three bacon slices—broken to fit sandwich comfortably
3. Place bread, spread on both sides on top. Add remaining bacon slices, onion rings, tomato slices, and lettuce pieces. Sprinkle black pepper lightly to taste on each layer as sandwich is made.
4. Top with remaining bread slice, spread side down. Secure layers of sandwich in place with toothpicks. Cut in half diagonally. Makes two sandwiches or one serving.

Nutrition Note: Substitute cold, cooked chicken or turkey frankfurters, sliced, for bacon, if desired.

DOUBLE DECKER ALTERNATIVE: CHEESE AND MUSHROOM

3 slices whole-wheat bread   1 to 2 tablespoons margarine

Filling

Shredded spinach leaves, or Chinese cabbage
½ cup skim-milk cottage cheese
¼ cup chopped mushrooms

¼ cup chopped parsley
½ to 1 teaspoon curry powder or dry mustard, to taste
2 to 4 slices boiled ham (2 ounces)

1. Toast bread, if desired. Spread margarine as directed in previous recipe.
2. Assemble sandwich as directed in previous recipe, layering half of spinach leaves, half of cottage cheese, mushrooms, parsley, a

sprinkling of curry powder, and half of ham slices.
3. Place middle slice bread in position; layer remaining filling ingredients, reversing their order.
4. Secure sandwich with toothpicks, as in previous recipe. Cut in half diagonally. Makes two sandwiches or one serving.

OVERSTUFFED CLUB ROLL SANDWICH

1 large individual club roll
1 tablespoon margarine

1 tablespoon prepared spicy mustard

Filling

¼ cup or more shredded Iceberg lettuce
4 to 6 cherry tomatoes, quartered
1 scallion stalk, finely sliced

2 thin slices cooked, rare, lean roast beef
Black pepper to taste

1. Cut top from roll; reserve. Using a teaspoon, hollow out soft crumbs from roll, leaving the crusty shell of the roll, about ¼-inch thick.
2. Blend margarine and mustard together. Spread over inside walls of roll and the cut surface of the top.
3. Place shredded lettuce at bottom of roll. Top with 2 or 3 cherry tomatoes, quartered, and half of sliced scallion. Roll beef slices and place, side by side, inside club roll. Cut beef rolls in half if necessary to fit.
4. Top with remaining cherry tomatoes, quartered, and with remaining sliced scallion. Sprinkle with black pepper to taste. Secure top of roll in place with toothpicks. Makes one serving.

CLUB ROLL SANDWICH ALTERNATIVE: APPLE AND PORK

1 large individual club roll
1 tablespoon margarine

1 tablespoon prepared spicy mustard

Filling

¼ cup finely shredded celery
¼ cup finely shredded apple
Lemon juice

2 to 3 thin slices cooked, lean pork
Powdered sage to taste

1. Prepare club roll as in previous recipe, spreading with margarine and mustard.
2. Toss celery and apple with a little lemon juice. Layer half inside roll. Top with rolled slices of pork and, finally, remaining apple-celery mixture.
3. As layers are being made sprinkle sandwich with a *little* powdered sage to taste. Secure top of roll in place with toothpicks. Makes one serving.

Nutrition Note: Once in a while beef and pork are necessary treats in the diet. Variety stimulates the appetite and it can not be ignored that both (while having saturated fat and cholesterol) are excellent sources of protein, iron and the vitamin B complex. Make sure the meats are lean, and eat occasionally. You can substitute chicken or turkey slices.

SUPER HERO

1 individual hero roll (about 6 to 8 inches long)
2 tablespoons olive oil
1 small garlic clove, crushed
½ teaspoon oregano, crumbled
½ teaspoon basil leaves, crumbled
¼ teaspoon black pepper

Filling

½ cup shredded Romaine or escarole lettuce
1 large tomato, thinly sliced
1 small onion, thinly sliced (optional)
½ green pepper, cut in julienne strips
½ sweet red pepper, cut in julienne strips
4 thin slices cooked, smoked turkey or chicken (about 2 ounces)
4 thin slices skim-milk Mozzarella cheese or Provalone cheese

1. Cut hero roll in half crosswise. In small custard cup, blend olive oil, garlic, oregano, basil, and black pepper. Brush or drizzle half of mixture on both cut surfaces of bread.
2. On bottom half of roll, layer half of shredded lettuce. Using half of tomato and half of onion slices, arrange alternately on top of lettuce. Using half of green and red pepper strips, place on top of tomato-onion layer. Drizzle with a little olive oil mixture.
3. Fold 2 turkey slices; place on top of green-red pepper layer. Top

with cheese. Layer remaining turkey, peppers, tomato and onion slices, and, finally, remaining shredded lettuce. Drizzle with remaining olive oil mixture. Place top of roll in place.
4. Secure sandwich by spearing with toothpicks so layers are firmly together. Or tie the sandwich with two or three loops of string. Makes one serving.

THE SWEDISH HERO ALTERNATIVE

1 individual hero roll (about 6 to 8 inches long)
2 tablespoons margarine, softened
2 teaspoons chopped fresh dill weed or 1 teaspoon dried

Filling

2 or 3 Boston lettuce leaves, torn in bite-size pieces
½ cup thin cucumber slices or zucchini slices
½ cup cup thin radish slices
4 thin slices salmon, whitefish, smoked turkey or 6 to 8 herring tidbits
Chopped fresh or dried dill weed
Red wine vinegar

1. Cut hero roll in half crosswise and spread with a blend of margarine and dill weed.
2. Using filling ingredients layer as in the Super Hero Sandwich, sprinkling each alternate layer with a few shreds of dill and drops of vinegar.
3. Secure top layer and base of sandwich as directed above. Makes one serving.

THE NONSANDWICH SUPER SANDWICH

Filling

2 tablespoons vegetable oil
½ cup onion slivers
1 6-ounce package frozen snow peas, thawed and cut in julienne strips
1 cup sliced mushrooms
½ cup sliced water chestnuts
1 cup cooked turkey (about ¼ pound) cut in julienne strips
2 teaspoons cornstarch
⅓ cup chicken broth
Grated lemon rind or grated fresh ginger root to taste
Black pepper to taste

Iceberg lettuce leaves

SUPER SANDWICHES 51

1. Make filling by heating oil in large skillet. Stir-fry onions for 1 minute. Add snow peas, mushrooms and water chestnuts. Stir-fry 2 minutes longer or until all vegetables are tender crusp. Add turkey. Stir-fry to heat meat throughly.
2. In small custard cup, blend cornstarch with chicken broth. Stir into vegetable-turkey mixture. Heat, stirring to thicken sauce and coat vegetables and turkey. Season to taste with lemon rind and black pepper. Let cool.
3. Using two or three lettuce leaves per cup, make two lettuce cups and divide filling between them. Roll lettuce around filling to contain, securing with toothpicks. Makes two lettuce super sandwiches or one serving.

Note: Brown baggers may prefer to pack filling and lettuce separately and make "sandwich" on the job. However, these can be made, wrapped individually in plastic wrap, and chilled overnight.

NONSANDWICH SUPER SANDWICH VARIATION: CHICKEN AND PINEAPPLE

Filling

2 tablespoons vegetable oil
½ cup 1-inch pieces scallion
½ cup celery in julienne strips
1 cup cooked chicken (about 4 ounces) in julienne strips
1 8-ounce can crushed pineapple in natural juices
2 teaspoons cornstarch
Red wine vinegar to taste
Brown sugar to taste

Iceberg lettuce leaves

1. Make filling by heating oil in large skillet. Stir-fry scallions and celery strips for 2 minutes. Add chicken. Stir-fry 1 to 2 minutes longer or until chicken is hot.
2. Drain juice from pineapple. In a small custard cup, blend juice with cornstarch. Stir into skillet. Heat to thicken sauce and coat vegetables and chicken. Stir in pineapple.
3. Add a little red wine vinegar and brown sugar to achieve sweet-sour flavor you prefer. Let cool.
4. Make lettuce cups as directed in previous recipe, filling and securing as directed. Makes two super sandwiches or one serving.

THE TORTILLA SANDWICH

2 soft, white-flour tortillas
1 tablespoon margarine

¼ teaspoon chili powder
2 drops hot pepper sauce

Filling

½ cup shredded Iceberg lettuce
1 medium tomato, diced and well drained (about ½ cup)
¼ cup shredded sharp Cheddar cheese

½ cup shredded, cooked chicken or turkey
Mexican hot sauce (salsa) to taste

1. Spread one side of each tortilla with margarine that has been blended with chili powder and hot pepper sauce.
2. On one tortilla, slightly lower than center, make band of half shredded lettuce; top with half of diced tomato, half of shredded cheese, and half of shredded chicken that has been moistened with a little Mexican hot sauce.
3. Fold bottom and sides of tortilla over filling and then roll up, jelly-roll fashion. Repeat, using second tortilla and remaining ingredients. Makes two tortillas or one serving.

Nutrition Note: Use shredded skim-milk mozzarella cheese as a Cheddar cheese alternative.

TORTILLA ALTERNATIVE

2 soft, white-flour tortillas

2 tablespoons creamy peanut butter

Filling

1 4-ounce can green chilies, drained and chopped
½ cup cold, cooked rice
1 clove garlic, crushed
½ teaspoon black pepper

1 to 2 tablespoons olive oil
1 to 2 teaspoons red wine vinegar
½ cup cooked, shredded turkey meat

1. Spread one side of each tortilla with peanut butter.
2. Make filling in medium bowl by blending chilies, rice, garlic, pepper, and enough olive oil and vinegar to moisten. Stir in turkey.

3. On one tortilla, slightly lower than center, make a band of half of filling. Fold bottom and sides of tortilla over filling and then roll up, jelly-roll fashion. Repeat, using second tortilla and remaining filling. Makes two tortillas or one serving.

TRIPLE DECKER SANDWICH—ORIENTAL STYLE

4 slices whole-wheat or your favorite bread
2 to 3 tablespoons margarine, softened
2 to 3 tablespoons sesame seeds, toasted if desired

Filling

Shredded spinach or dark leaf lettuce
1 8-ounce can water chestnuts, drained and thinly sliced
1 2-ounce jar pimientos, drained and chopped
½ cup diced, cooked chicken
¼ cup slivered almonds
Low-fat, unflavored yogurt
Grated lemon rind, to taste
Powdered ginger, to taste

1. Toast bread, if desired. Blend margarine and sesame seeds. Spread one side of two slices bread and both sides of remaining two slices bread.
2. Set one slice of bread spread side uppermost and top with half of shredded spinach, water chestnuts, and pimientos. Place bread slice with spread on both sides on top.
3. Blend together chicken, almonds, yogurt just to moisten, and lemon rind and ginger to taste. Spread on top of bread slice as middle layer of sandwich. Cover with second slice of bread with spread on both sides.
4. Top with pimientos, water chestnuts, and shredded spinach. Set remaining bread slice, spread side down, on top. Secure layers of sandwich in place with long toothpicks. Cut in half diagonally. Makes two sandwiches or one serving.

ITALIAN TRIPLE DECKER ALTERNATIVE

4 slices whole-wheat or your favorite bread
2 to 3 tablespoons margarine, softened
2 to 3 tablespoons grated Parmesan cheese

BROWN BAG LUNCHES

Filling

Thin zucchini slices
Thin shreds fennel or celery
4 to 6 thin slices Mozzarella cheese (2 ounces)
1 medium-size tomato, thinly sliced

1 to 2 tablespoons finely shredded fresh basil or 1½ to 2 teaspoons crumbled dried basil leaves
Black pepper
Olive oil and red wine vinegar, to taste

1. Toast bread, if desired. Blend together margarine and cheese. Spread slices as directed in previous recipe.
2. Assemble sandwich as directed in previous recipe. The first layer is of thin zucchini slices and fennel. The middle layer is of Mozzarella and tomato slices arranged alternately and overlapping and sprinkled with basil, black pepper, olive oil, and vinegar to taste. The third layer is thin zucchini slices and fennel.
3. Secure sandwich with toothpicks as in previous recipe. Cut in half diagonally. Makes two sandwiches or one serving.

THE PITA SANDWICH

1 6-inch whole-wheat pita bread

Filling

½ cup crumbled feta cheese (about 2 ounces)
or
½ cup finely diced skim-milk Mozzarella cheese (about 2 ounces)
1 small tomato, diced and well drained

¼ cup diced, unpeeled zucchini
¼ cup diced green pepper
2 tablespoons finely chopped onion

Dressing

1 8-ounce can chickpeas (garbanzo beans), drained and crushed
3 to 4 tablespoons olive oil
2 to 3 tablespoons red wine vinegar

1 clove garlic, crushed
½ teaspoon crushed thyme leaves

1. Cut edge of pita bread so it may be stuffed.
2. Make filling by tossing together feta cheese, tomato, zucchini, green pepper, and onion.
3. Make dressing by stirring togehter crushed chickpeas, enough olive oil and vinegar to make into a creamy consistency, and garlic and thyme.
4. Stir only enough dressing into filling to barely moisten and bind ingredients together. (Refrigerate remaining dressing for another use.) Place filling inside pita bread. Makes one serving.

VEGETARIAN PITA ALTERNATIVE

1 6-inch whole-wheat pita bread

Filling

1 8-ounce can red kidney beans, well-drained
¼ cup thinly slivered, fresh green beans
¼ cup crumbled feta cheese or skim-milk cottage cheese
¼ cup chopped parsley
2 tablespoons pine nuts or toasted sesame seeds
2 tablespoons finely chopped onion

Dressing

1 8-ounce can chickpeas (garbanzo beans), drained and crushed
3 to 4 tablespoons olive oil
2 to 3 tablespoons red wine vinegar
1 clove garlic, crushed
½ teaspoon crushed thyme leaves

1. Cut edge of pita bread so it may be stuffed.
2. Make filling by blending together kidney beans, green beans, feta cheese, parsley, pine nuts, and onion. Moisten and bind together with dressing (recipe above).
3. Place filling inside pita bread. Makes one serving.

Note: For brown baggers—pack bread and moistened filling separately; combine just before eating.

Nutrition Note: Rinse Feta cheese under cold water to remove brine; pat dry on paper towels.

STUFFED JELLY-ROLL SANDWICHES

4 thin slices enriched white bread or whole-wheat bread

1 to 2 tablespoons margarine, softened

Filling

1 8-ounce can chickpeas (garbanzo beans), rinsed and drained
½ cup crumbled feta cheese or skim-milk cottage cheese
½ cup finely grated carrot
1 to 2 cloves garlic, crushed
Black pepper to taste

1. Trim crusts from bread. Place bread slices between two large sheets waxed paper or plastic wrap. Roll with a rolling pin. Spread each slice lightly with margarine.
2. Make filling in blender or food processor by pureeing chickpeas. Stir in cheese, carrots, adding garlic and black pepper to taste. Filling should be semifirm (if not, add 2 or 3 tablespoons fresh bread crumbs.)
3. Divide filling between bread slices, place in a compact line at one end of bread. Roll up each slice jelly-roll fashion. Place each in plastic wrap or foil. Chill. Makes four sandwiches or one serving.

Nutrition Note: Feta cheese, while a good source of protein, vitamins A and D, and calcium, is brine-packed. Rinse well before using, patting dry. And use only occasionally as a flavor treat. Skim-milk cottage cheese is the more nutritionally beneficial product.

4
FINGER-LICKIN' FOOD

There are some lunch box foods that are just best eaten out-of-hand. Cold chicken, ribs, chicken pies, and corn dogs are crisp and savory treats on which to feast. So pack a couple of extra paper napkins, and a damp paper towel in a plastic bag, and be prepared to eat the best of traditional picnic food.

Best of all, here are practical recipes to be used as a meal the night before, with leftovers planned for the next day's lunch. Or cook up a batch of barbeque ribs—or any similar finger-lickin' food—then freeze in individual portions to use when needed.

Make no doubt about it, most of these dishes are sometime, not everyday, treats. Traditional cold lunch box foods such as these do not always have the complete nutritional contents today's brown bagger wants, so a fresh salad should be packed along with them.

NUTRITIONAL KNOW-HOW:
- These recipes skillfully reduce fat by suggesting that chicken and turkey frankfurters be used instead of beef or pork.
- Similarly, ground raw turkey meat makes a good alternate to bulk sausage meat.
- Boiling and then roasting pork, beef, and lamb ribs ensures that much of their fat is drained away.
- Pastry, a once-in-a-while treat, is made with whole-wheat flour and enriched cornmeal.
- All recipes have either a meat or dairy protein as their own nutritional attribute. Meats have iron and the vitamin B complex as part of their nutritional profile; dairy foods are excellent sources of vitamins A and D.
- However, make most of your choices from "lean" meats, especially chicken and turkey, and low-fat products. And current dietary guidelines recommend that there be no more than 4 eggs eaten each week.

Consumer Notes on Finger-Lickin' Foods

All foods based on meat and dairy products need special care in cooking and packing.

- Make sure that all perishable protein foods are purchased fresh (check open dating where possible) and from a clean supplier.
- Double check that surfaces and utensils are clean during preparation and that cooking temperatures are accurate and cooking times long enough.
- Once cooked, cool foods as quickly as possible. Cover, chill, and then wrap individually for the lunch box.
- Place in an *insulated* lunch box. Any leftovers should be discarded once they are returned home. These should not be served to anyone after being in a lunch box all day.

Pack meat safely by wrapping in plastic wrap or foil and putting in a separate container from other food. Pastry shoud be placed in a noncrushable container.

BARBECUED RIBS

1 3-pound side pork spare ribs, cut into 2-rib portions

Water

Barbecue Sauce

1 tablespoon vegetable oil
¼ cup finely chopped onion
1 clove garlic, crushed
½ cup tomato ketchup
¼ cup honey
¼ cup cider vinegar
2 tablespoons grated lemon rind

1 teaspoon finely chopped fresh ginger root or ½ teaspoon powdered ginger
½ to ¾ teaspoon hot pepper sauce

1. Place spare ribs in large Dutch oven or saucepan; cover with cold water. Simmer, covered, 1 hour or until tender. Drain from water and cool.
2. To make sauce: In a medium skillet, heat oil. Cook onion and garlic until tender, stirring constantly, about 5 minutes. Stir in ketchup, honey, vinegar, lemon rind, ginger, and hot pepper sauce. Simmer, uncovered, stirring occasionally until sauce coats back of spoon, about 10 minutes.
3. Preheat oven to 425°F. Place ribs in single layer in roasting pan, brushing on all sides with barbecue sauce. Bake 30 to 40 minutes or until crisp and brown, brushing after 15 minutes with any remaining sauce and pan drippings. Makes four servings.

Nutrition Note: Pork is a good source of protein and B vitamins. Simmering and roasting removes most of the fat.

DEVILED BEEF RIBS

3 pounds beef ribs, cut in 2-inch pieces	1 onion, quartered
	1 bay leaf
Water	1 teaspoon thyme leaves

Deviled Sauce

½ cup tomato ketchup	1 to 2 cloves garlic, crushed
½ cup prepared mild mustard	¼ to ½ teaspoon hot pepper sauce
2 tablespoons prepared horse-radish	

1. Place beef ribs in large Dutch oven or saucepan; cover with cold water. Add onion, bay leaf, and thyme leaves. Simmer, covered, 45 minutes or until tender. Drain from water and cool.
2. Make sauce: In small saucepan, combine ketchup, mustard, horse-radish, garlic, and hot pepper sauce. Simmer, uncovered, to blend flavors, about 5 minutes.
3. Preheat oven to 375°F. Place ribs in single layer in roasting pan, brushing on all sides with deviled sauce. Bake 30 minutes or until crisp and brown, brushing every 10 minutes with remaining sauce and pan drippings. Makes four servings.

Nutrition Note: Beef is a good source of protein, iron, and B vitamins. For some people, its fat content may make it only an occasional treat in the diet; however, simmering and roasting does remove much of the fat.

CHICKEN CHEESE ROLLUPS

2 7½-ounce packages of refrigerator biscuits	⅔ cup grated sharp Cheddar cheese or any firm skim-milk cheese, grated
10 chicken or beef frankfurters	⅔ cup grated onion

1. Preheat oven to 375°F. Place 2 biscuits end to end on floured surface; press dough together and roll into rectangle large enough to wrap around a frankfurter.

2. Sprinkle 1 tablespoon grated cheese over dough, then sprinkle with 1 tablespoon grated onion. Place frankfurter on top; dampen edges of dough. Bring dough up and around frankfurters, pinch well to seal.
3. Place on ungreased baking sheet; bake 12 to 15 minutes or until golden brown. Makes four servings.

Nutrition Note: Whole-wheat Pastry, page 63, may be used instead of refrigerator biscuits.

CHILI CHICKEN DOGS

2 tablespoons vegetable oil
1 cup chopped onion
1 clove garlic, crushed
½ to 1 teaspoon chili powder
¼ cup brown sugar, firmly packed
½ cup tomato juice
2 tablespoons tomato paste
2 tablespoons red wine vinegar
8 chicken frankfurters (1 pound)

1. In small saucepan heat oil, and cook onions and garlic, stirring constantly until tender, about 5 to 7 minutes. Stir in chili powder; cook 1 minute longer.
2. Add brown sugar, tomato juice, tomato paste, and red wine vinegar. Simmer, covered, 10 minutes or until onions are very tender and sauce is a thick purée. Add more tomato juice to prevent sticking.
3. Preheat oven to 400°F. Place frankfurters in roasting pan. Bake 5 minutes. Brush with sauce; bake 15 minutes longer, brushing frequently with sauce and pan drippings. Cool and spear each frankfurter lengthwise with wooden ice cream stick for easy holding. Wrap individually in plastic wrap or foil, chilling until time to pack. Makes four servings.

CHICKEN CORN DOGS

Whole-wheat — Corn Pastry

1 cup all-purpose flour
½ cup whole-wheat flour
½ cup yellow corn meal
½ teaspoon salt (optional)
⅔ cup margarine
¼ cup water

8 chicken frankfurters, precooked and cooled

1. In large bowl, combine all-purpose flour, whole-wheat flour and corn meal; add salt if desired. Using two knives or a pastry cutter, cut in margarine until mixture resembles coarse crumbs. Sprinkle over water; gently knead mixture together with finger tips to form a soft dough. Chill.
2. Preheat oven to 400°F. Divide dough into 8 pieces. Roll out each, on a lightly floured surface, into a rectangle just large enough to cover each frankfurter. Dampen all edges.
3. Roll dough up to cover and contain frankfurter. Press dampened edges to seal. Place on ungreased baking sheet. Bake 20 to 25 minutes until crisp and golden brown. Makes four servings.

APPLE-GLAZED LAMB RIBLETS

3 pounds lamb riblets, cut into 2-rib serving pieces

Water

Apple Glaze

¾ cup unsweetened apple sauce
1 small seedless orange, cut into small chunks

¼ **cup vegetable oil**
1 1-inch piece fresh ginger root or 1 teaspoon powdered ginger

1. Place lamb riblets in large Dutch oven or saucepan; cover with cold water. Simmer, covered, 45 minutes or until tender. Drain from water and cool.
2. To make glaze: In blender container or food processor combine apple sauce, orange cut in chunks (including rind), vegetable oil, and fresh ginger. Blend or process to make a smooth glaze.
3. Preheat oven to 425°F. Place ribs in single layer in roasting pan, brushing on all sides with apple glaze. Bake 30 to 40 minutes or until crisp and brown, brushing after 15 minutes with any remaining glaze. Makes four servings.

Nutrition Note: You may use 2 pounds chicken wings, substituting for lamb riblets and simmering only 10 minutes.

CRISP COLD CHICKEN

1 broiler-frying chicken, cut up (2½ to 3 pounds)
1 8-ounce carton low-fat, unflavored yogurt
2 teaspoons grated lemon rind

Coating

1 cup dry, unseasoned breadcrumbs
¼ cup grated Parmesan cheese
1½ teaspoons crushed basil leaves
1½ teaspoon crushed oregano
¼ teaspoon black pepper

1. Wipe chicken with damp paper towels. Cut into 6 or 8 serving pieces. Ideally there should be 2 drumsticks, 2 thighs and each breast half divided (if large enough) into 2 pieces.
2. Beat together yogurt and lemon rind. Place in shallow glass baking dish. Add chicken pieces, turning to coat well. Let stand at room temperature 45 minutes, turning frequently; or cover and refrigerate up to 24 hours.
3. To make coating: In a large plastic bag combine breadcrumbs, cheese, basil, oregano, and pepper. Drain 2 pieces of chicken at a time from yogurt. Place in plastic bag and shake well to coat.
4. Preheat oven to 400°F. Place chicken in single layer on shallow roasting pan. Bake 45 minutes or until tender and juices run clear when pierced with fork. Makes four servings.

PICNIC CHICKEN DRUMSTICKS

2 pounds (about 8 to 10) chicken drumsticks
1 tablespoon grated lemon rind
½ teaspoon black pepper

Sweet-Sour Glaze

1 8-ounce can apricot halves in water, drained
2 tablespoons lemon juice
2 tablespoons vegetable oil
2 tablespoons honey

1. Preheat oven to 375°F. Wipe chicken drumsticks with damp paper towels. Mix together lemon rind and black pepper, use to season each drumstick.
2. Place drumsticks in single layer in roasting pan. Roast 15 minutes.
3. Meanwhile, make glaze: In blender container purée apricot halves, lemon juice, vegetable oil, and honey. Brush over drumsticks to coat well. Roast 20 to 25 minutes longer, brushing once more with any remaining sauce and pan drippings. Chicken is done when juices run clear. Makes four servings.

VERY SPICY CHICKEN WINGS

2 pounds chicken wings (about 12 wings)
½ cup vegetable oil
2 tablespoons red wine vinegar
1 to 2 tablespoons hot pepper sauce

1. Wipe chicken wings with damp paper towels. Trim off tips and fold wings so they form a triangle.
2. In large bowl beat together vegetable oil, vinegar, and hot pepper sauce. Add wings, and toss well to coat.
3. Preheat oven to 375°F. Place wings in single layer in roasting pan. Bake 30 to 40 minutes until very golden and crisp. Baste with any remaining oil, hot pepper sauce mixture, and pan drippings while roasting. Makes four servings.

CORNISH PASTRIES

Whole-wheat Pastry

1 cup all-purpose flour
1 cup whole-wheat flour
⅓ cup margarine
⅓ cup solid vegetable shortening
½ teaspoon salt (optional)
¼ cup water

Filling

1 pound ground beef or ground raw turkey meat
½ cup finely chopped onion
½ cup finely diced carrots
½ cup finely diced celery
¾ teaspoon crumbled thyme leaves
½ teaspoon black pepper

1. To make pastry: Place flour in large bowl; using two knives or a pastry cutter, cut in margarine and vegetable shortening. Add salt, if desired. Sprinkle with water; using finger tips, press dough together to form a ball. Chill until ready to use.
2. To make filling: In large skillet over medium heat, cook beef, stirring to break into small pieces. As fat begins to flow, add onion, carrots, and celery. Sprinkle with thyme and pepper. Cook, stirring constantly, 10 minutes. Cool completely. (If using ground raw turkey meat, add 2 tablespoons vegetable oil to skillet to cook meat.)
3. Divide pastry into 4 pieces. On a lightly floured surface roll each out into a 5-inch circle. Dampen edges of each circle. Place one-fourth filling in center of each. Fold over pastry to cover; press and roll edges to seal. Chill while oven is preheating.
4. Preheat oven to 425°F. Place Cornish Pastries on an ungreased baking sheet. Bake 20 to 25 minutes or until pastry is golden-brown and crisp. Makes four servings.

Nutrition Note: Pastry can be made by using all margarine for the shortening.

COUNTRY CAPTAIN PIES

3 cups cooked, diced chicken
¾ cup dark raisins, coarsely chopped
½ cup slivered almonds
1 cup chopped diced tomato (1 large tomato)
¼ cup chopped parsley
½ to 1 teaspoon curry powder
Whole-wheat Pastry—see recipe page 63

1. In medium bowl combine cooked, diced chicken, raisins, almonds, and tomato and any juice. Stir in parsley and curry powder to taste.
2. Preheat oven to 425°F. Make Whole-wheat Pastry as directed for Cornish Pastries, page 63.
3. Divide pastry into 4 pieces. On lightly floured surface, roll each out into 5-inch circle. Dampen edges of each circle. Place one-fourth filling in center of each. Fold over pastry to cover; press and roll edges to seal.
4. Place Country Captain Pies on an ungreased baking sheet. Bake 20 to 25 minutes or until pastry is crisp and golden-brown. Makes four servings.

EGG ROLLS

Filling

¼ cup margarine
1 cup finely shredded cabbage
½ cup chopped scallions
½ cup chopped water chestnuts

1 cup cooked, shredded chicken
2 eggs, beaten
¼ teaspoon black pepper

8 egg roll skins

Beaten egg, or 1 teaspoon cornstarch plus 1 tablespoon water

1. In medium skillet melt margarine; add cabbage, scallions, and water chestnuts. Stir to combine; cook, covered, over low heat so vegetables steam tender, about 3 to 5 minutes. Stir in shredded chicken.
2. Raise heat to medium-high. Add beaten egg in a thin stream, stirring mixture in skillet rapidly so egg cooks and breaks into small pieces. Sprinkle with pepper. Cool filling completely.
3. Divide filling evenly among 8 egg roll skins, placing filling in a band, slightly below the center of the dough.
4. Roll up dough to contain filling, turning sides in toward center to hold filling firmly. Seal edges of dough with additional beaten egg or cornstarch-water paste. Chill while oven is preheating.
5. Preheat oven to 425°F. Brush egg rolls lightly with oil to coat. Bake 25 to 30 minutes until dough is crisp and golden-brown. Makes four servings.

SCOTCH EGGS

4 hard-cooked eggs
Flour
1 pound ground-raw turkey meat
½ cup dry, seasoned bread crumbs

2 tablespoons vegetable oil
1 egg, beaten
2 tablespoons water
1½ cups crushed, ready-to-eat, crisp whole-wheat cereal

1. Peel and cool hard-cooked eggs to room temperature, but do not chill. Dust eggs lightly with flour to coat; set aside.
2. Mix turkey meat, bread crumbs, and oil. Divide into 4 even pieces. On a lightly floured surface, press or roll each piece into a 3-inch circle.
3. Place egg in center of each turkey meat circle. Dampen edges, then lift up turkey meat to enclose each egg, rolling each coated egg on lightly floured surface till turkey meat coating is firmly in place.
4. Preheat oven to 425°F. Beat together egg and water; place crushed cereal in plastic bag. Brush egg mixture over sausage-meat-coated egg, and place cooked egg in bag containing cereal; shake to coat. Repeat to coat all Scotch Eggs.
5. Bake 30 to 35 minutes until turkey meat coating is crisp and golden brown. Cool completely and chill before packing. Makes four servings.

Nutrition Note: Instead of traditional high-fat sausage meat, we have used raw, ground turkey meat. This should be an occasional lunch box dish since eggs are high in cholesterol.

FOUR FABULOUS PIES

Whole-wheat Pastry—recipe page 63

Tuna-Celery Filling

1 7½-ounce can water-packed tuna, drained
½ cup finely chopped celery
½ cup chopped black olives
¼ cup chopped parsley
2 tablespoons grated onion
1 to 2 tablespoons prepared, spicy mustard

1. In medium bowl flake tuna; combine with celery, black olives, parsley, onion, and prepared mustard. Divide among 4 5-inch pastry circles.
2. Dampen edges, fold pastry over to contain filling, and seal and roll edges. Bake in preheated 425°F oven for 20 to 25 minutes. Makes four servings.

Spinach and Cheese Filling

1 pound fresh spinach leaves
2 8-ounce cartons low-fat, small-curd cottage cheese
2 teaspoons grated lemon rind
¼ teaspoon nutmeg
1 egg, beaten

1. Wash spinach well, discarding stems and discolored leaves. Place in saucepan without water and cook, covered, over low heat 3 to 5 minutes, or until spinach is tender. Drain, pressing to remove liquid. Chop finely.
2. Place spinach in bowl; stir in small-curd cheese, lemon rind, nutmeg, and beaten egg. Divide filling among four 5-inch pastry circles; proceed and bake as above.

All-Vegetable Filling

15-ounce can chickpeas (garbanzo beans)
2 tablespoons vegetable oil
½ cup chopped onion
2 cloves garlic, crushed
1 cup grated carrot
½ cup finely chopped green pepper
¼ cup chopped parsley

1. Rinse chickpeas; drain and place in medium bowl. Using a potato masher or fork, crush chickpeas to a coarse puree. (You could do this with a food processor, but not a blender.)
2. In medium skillet, in hot oil, cook onions and garlic until tender, about 5 minutes. Add carrot, green pepper, and parsley; cook 3 minutes more. Stir in chickpeas; cool completely. Divide filling among four 5-inch pastry circles, proceed and bake as above.

Broccoli-Walnut Filling

1 pound broccoli spears
½ cup coarsely broken walnut pieces
2 tablespoons margarine
2 tablespoons chopped dill weed or 2 teaspoons dried dill weed
1 tablespoon lemon juice
1 teaspoon grated lemon rind

1. Cut broccoli into flowerets and stems into ¼-inch thick slices. Cook, covered, in ½ inch boiling water until tender, about 12 to 15 minutes. Drain and chop coarsely.
2. Add walnut pieces, margarine, dill, lemon juice, and lemon rind; cool completely. Divide among four 5-inch pastry circles; proceed and bake as above.

EMPANADAS
(Mexican Meat Pies)

2 tablespoons vegetable oil
1 cup chopped onion
1 clove garlic, crushed
1 cup chopped, diced tomato (1 large tomato)
½ cup chopped green olives
¼ cup dark raisins, chopped
¼ cup chopped almonds
¼ cup chopped parsley
2 tablespoons capers, drained
2 cups cooked, shredded chicken
Whole-wheat Pastry—see recipe page 63

1. In medium skillet heat oil. Cook onion and garlic until tender, stirring constantly, about 5 minutes. Stir in tomato and liquid, olives, raisins, almonds, parsley, and capers. Heat over low heat 2 minutes to blend flavors. Stir in shredded chicken. Cool mixture completely.
2. Preheat oven to 425°F. Make Whole-wheat Pastry as directed for Cornish Pastries, page 63.
3. Divide pastry into 4 pieces. On lightly floured surface, roll each out into 5-inch circle. Dampen edges of each circle. Place one-fourth filling in center of each. Fold over pastry to cover; press and roll edges to seal.
4. Place empanadas on ungreased baking sheet. Bake 20 to 25 minutes or until pastry is crisp and golden brown. Makes four servings.

SAUSAGE ROLLS

1 8-ounce package brown-and-serve sausages
1 7½-ounce package refrigerated crescent rolls
1 tablespoon prepared, spicy mustard

1. Cook brown-and-serve sausages according to package directions. Cool completely.
2. Preheat oven to 425°F. Unroll refrigerated crescent rolls and divide into 8 pieces. Spread each dough section lightly with mustard. Place sausage at widest end of each section and roll up towards tip.
3. Bake 10 to 12 minutes or until dough is golden brown. Cook completely and chill before packing. Makes four servings.

Nutrition Note: Chicken frankfurters may be used instead of sausage. Cook according to package directions before using as above.

5
THE BIG MAIN-DISH SALAD

A hearty salad containing cold meat or fish or cheese or eggs is a good alternate to a sandwich, soup, or stew as the focus of the brown bagger's lunch—especially when the weather is hot.

Main dish salads are impractical to make in one-serving portions. We suggest making a 4-serving recipe, having the larger portion for dinner the evening before and reserving a portion for lunch the next day. Of course, there are several solutions for using up a big main-dish salad: you may have more than one brown bagger to provide for; many of the salads will keep safely in the refrigerator up to 24 hours to be featured in the lunch box a second day; and you can divide the recipe in half to make a smaller portion. All these suggestions are in the interests of practicality, ease, and economy. Use the solution best for your meal-style.

NUTRITION KNOW-HOW:

A salad a day does keep the doctor away—and for the following reasons:
- Raw vegetables and leafy salad makings are an excellent source of fiber.
- Dark green leafy vegetables such as spinach are a good source of vitamin A and some, such as cabbage, are also a good source of vitamin C.
- Orange-colored vegetables such as carrots are an excellent source of vitamin A, too. And tomatoes provide a beneficial amount of vitamin C.
- Many traditional salad meats and other protein ingredients contain saturated fat and/or a cholesterol content that should be in the diet sparingly. Thus, these recipes feature turkey, chicken, and tuna packed in water, rather than oil, and skim-milk cheeses.
- An occasional luxury recipe featuring ham or beef is included, but the prudent brown bagger will make these *only* occasionally. Or else he or she will substitute one of the leaner, lower-fat proteins.
- Salt is always to be added at the discretion of the brown bagger. We prefer to substitute grated lemon rind and pungent spicy herbs for salt.

- In dressings, low-fat, unflavored yogurt is prefered. You can use mayonnaise or sour cream occasionally. Better yet, look for calorie- and fat-reduced versions of these products.

Consumer Know-How and Tips on Salads
- Buy fresh produce, store it properly, and use it up quickly to insure maximum vitamin content.
- In the interests of time and convenience, most of these main dish salads can be made ahead and stored overnight.
- When it is recommended to add dressing at the last minute, do precisely that; otherwise the salad will be soggy.

For food safety discard all salads if uneaten. All main-dish salads should be kept chilled in firm containers until the moment they are packed. Then place the salad and its container in an *insulated* lunch box.

HEARTY CAESAR SALAD

1 large head Romaine lettuce
1 cup garlic-flavored croutons
8 ounces Monterey Jack cheese, cubed (about 2 cups)
¼ cup grated Parmesan cheese

Dressing

½ cup olive oil
¼ cup lemon juice
1 tablespoon prepared Dijon-style mustard
4 anchovy fillets, chopped (optional)
1 teaspoon grated lemon rind
¼ teaspoon black pepper

1. Tear Romaine lettuce into bite-size pieces; place in large salad bowl. Toss with garlic-flavored croutons and cheese, and sprinkle with Parmesan cheese. Cover and chill until serving time.
2. Make dressing by beating oil, lemon juice, mustard, and anchovy fillets, if desired, and lemon rind and black pepper. Chill until serving time. Pour dressing over salad and toss to serve. Makes four servings.

Note for brown baggers: Place 1½ cups salad in salad container. Place 3 tablespoons dressing in smaller, tight-seal container. Chill both overnight. Combine just before eating. Garlic croutons can be store-bought or homemade.

Nutrition Note: This is a less-than-traditional salad since the dressing contains no raw egg—unsafe for a brown bag lunch. However, you may wish to replace half the cheese by substituting 2 hard-cooked eggs, coarsely chopped.

THE HEALTHY CHEF'S SALAD

1 small head Boston lettuce
1 small head escarole lettuce
3 medium-size tomatoes, cut in thin wedges
4 ounces cooked chicken, cut in julienne strips (about 1 cup)
4 ounces cooked turkey, cut in julienne strips (about 1 cup)
2 ounces skim-milk Mozzarella cheese, cubed (about ½ cup)

Dressing

⅓ cup vegetable oil
¼ cup lemon juice
2 tablespoons finely snipped fresh dill weed or 1 tablespoon dried dill weed
2 teaspoons grated lemon rind
1 clove garlic, crushed
½ teaspoon black pepper

1. Tear Boston and escarole lettuce into large, bite-size pieces. Place in large serving bowl; toss gently with tomatoes, chicken, turkey, and Mozzarella, just to combine. Cover and chill.
2. Make dressing by beating oil, lemon juice, dill, lemon rind, garlic, and black pepper to combine. Chill until serving time. Pour dressing over salad and toss to serve. Makes four servings.

Note for brown baggers: Place 2 cups salad in large salad container. Place ¼ cup dressing in smaller, tight-seal container. Chill both overnight. Combine just before eating.

Nutrition Note: The traditional chef's salad usually contains Swiss cheese, ham, and hard-cooked eggs. These high-fat/high cholesterol ingredients have been replaced by ingredients much more acceptable to the nutrition conscious brown bagger.

COTTAGE CHEESE AND FRUIT SALAD

- 1 8-ounce container low-fat cottage cheese
- ½ cup coarsely chopped, dry-roasted, unsalted peanuts
- 2 tablespoons toasted sesame seeds
- 1 cup cubed cantaloupe melon
- 1 cup sliced strawberries
- 2 seedless oranges
- 2 tablespoons lemon juice
- 1 tablespoon honey
- ½ teaspoon grated lemon rind

1. In small bowl blend cottage cheese, peanuts and sesame seeds. Mound in center of salad platter.
2. In medium bowl gently toss together melon cubes and strawberries. Use sharp knife to remove orange peel, cutting off rind and pith. Cut between the membranes on each side of every segment to free sections. Add to fruit mixture.
3. In small custard cup beat together lemon juice, honey, and lemon rind. Drizzle over fruit; toss to combine. Spoon fruit around cottage cheese. Chill until serving time. Makes four servings.

Note for brown baggers: Place one-fourth cheese mixture in a salad container. Place fruit mixture in a second container. Chill overnight.

CALIFORNIA CHICKEN SALAD

- 2 medium-size red grapefruit
- 2 large seedless oranges
- 8 ounces cooked chicken, cut in ½-inch cubes (about 2 cups)
- ½ cup toasted, slivered almonds
- 2 tablespoons snipped chives

Dressing

- ¼ cup olive oil
- 2 tablespoons lemon juice
- 1 teaspoon grated orange rind
- ½ teaspoon grated lemon rind
- ⅛ teaspoon black pepper

1 large bunch watercress or curly chickory

1. Cut peel from grapefruits to remove both the rind and the white pith. Similarly remove peel from oranges. Cut between the membranes on each side of every segment to free sections. Place grapefruit and orange segments in a large bowl.
2. Add chicken, almonds, and chives to bowl. Toss gently to com-

bine. Make dressing in a glass measuring cup by beating together olive oil, lemon juice, grated orange and lemon rind, and black pepper. Pour over salad ingredients; toss gently to combine.
3. Chill salad at least 1 hour. Place on platter lined with watercress sprigs or curly chickory. Makes four servings.

Note for brown baggers: Place one-fourth of salad in salad container. Separately place watercress sprigs or chickory in plastic container. Chill overnight. Eat salad greens along with chicken salad.

CHICKEN, PASTA, AND VEGETABLE SALAD

8 ounces uncooked, thin spaghetti or linguine

2 tablespoons peanut oil

Dressing

⅔ cup creamy peanut butter
⅓ cup cider vinegar
¼ cup soy sauce
3 to 4 tablespoons water, or more

2 cloves garlic, crushed
6 drops hot pepper sauce, or to taste

8 ounces cooked chicken, cubed (about 2 cups)
1 cup thinly sliced celery, cut on the diagonal

1 cup grated carrots
¼ cup finely chopped, dry-roasted, unsalted peanuts

1. Cook spaghetti according to package directions, until "al dente"—just tender. Drain well; toss with peanut oil. Set aside to cool to room temperature.
2. Make dressing in a small bowl by stirring together peanut butter, cider vinegar, and soy sauce. Stir in water to achieve a soft, pouring consistency. Stir in garlic and hot pepper sauce, adjusting seasoning to taste.
3. Pour dressing over spaghetti; toss to combine. Place in serving bowl. Top spaghetti with a layer of chicken, then celery and carrots. Sprinkle peanuts on top. Chill until serving time. Toss the salad to blend just before serving. Makes four servings.

Note for brown baggers: Place 1½ cups salad in salad container. Chill overnight.

HERBED CHICKEN AND WHEAT SALAD

1 cup bulgar wheat
Water
1 cup finely chopped parsley
1 cup finely chopped scallions
½ cup finely chopped mint
2 teaspoons grated lemon rind
½ teaspoon black pepper
½ cup olive oil
¼ cup lemon juice
2 medium size tomatoes, peeled, seeded, and diced
8 ounces pre-cooked chicken, cut in julienne strips (2 cups)
Romaine lettuce leaves

1. Place bulgar wheat in a large bowl; add water to a depth of 1-inch above the bulgar wheat. Let stand 1 hour. Place wheat in a fine colander or strainer and press gently to remove excess water.
2. Return wheat to bowl; add parsley, scallions, mint, lemon rind, and black pepper. Toss to blend well. Stir in olive oil and lemon juice; cover and chill at least 1 hour for flavors to blend.
3. Prepare tomatoes, draining off any excess juice. Add to bulgar-wheat mixture together with chicken. Serve on Romaine lettuce leaves, if desired. Makes four servings.

Note for brown baggers: Place one-fourth salad in salad container. Chill overnight. Pack lettuce leaves separately.

SPICY CHICKPEA SAUSAGE SALAD

10 hot Italian sausages (about 1 pound)
1 20-ounce can chickpeas, rinsed and well-drained
2 cloves garlic, crushed
2 tablespoons fresh lemon juice
2 teaspoons grated lemon rind
½ teaspoon black pepper
½ cup black olives, cut in half
¼ cup chopped parsley

1. Prick Italian sausage thoroughly; place in large skillet over low heat. Cook, covered, 15 to 20 minutes or until well cooked, turning frequently. Drain and cool sausages; cut crosswise into slices.
2. In food processor or blender, combine chickpeas, garlic, lemon juice, lemon rind, and black pepper. Process briefly, just to break up beans.
3. Stir in sliced sausage, black olives, and parsley. Serve on lettuce leaf lined plate if desired. Makes four servings.

Note for brown baggers: Place one-fourth of salad mixture in a salad container; chill overnight.

Nutrition Note: Substitute chicken frankfurters for hot Italian sausages, if desired. You may wish to compensate for the lack of hot seasoning by adding 6 drops hot pepper sauce.

LAYERED CHILI SALAD

- ¾ pound ground beef
- ½ cup finely chopped onion
- 2 cloves garlic, crushed
- 1 to 3 teaspoons chili powder
- ⅓ cup vegetable oil
- 2 tablespoons red wine vinegar
- 1 8-ounce can chickpeas (garbanzo beans), rinsed and drained
- 1 cup finely shredded Iceberg lettuce
- 2 medium size tomatoes, coarsely chopped
- ½ cup chopped green chilies, (optional)
- ½ cup chopped cilantro (Chinese parsley) or parsley

1. In medium skillet over low heat cook beef, stirring constantly. As meat juices flow, add onion, garlic, and chili powder. Stir constantly to break up meat, and cook thoroughly. Drain off any surplus fat.
2. Add oil and vinegar to skillet. Stir well; let cool to room temperature. Place meat in 9-inch square glass casserole.
3. Top meat with a layer of beans, and lettuce. Chop tomatoes (peeling and seeding if desired), drain free of juices, and layer on top of lettuce. Sprinkle with chilies, if desired, and cilantro. Chill before serving. Makes four servings.

Note for brown baggers: Using one-fourth of all salad ingredients, layer in large salad container as above. Chill overnight.

Nutrition Note: Raw ground turkey meat may be used as a substitute for beef.

EGG AND ASPARAGUS SALAD WITH CREAMY DRESSING

4 hard-cooked eggs

1½ pounds fresh asparagus (about 20 to 24 spears)

Dressing

1 cup low-fat, unflavored yogurt or mayonnaise
¼ cup grated Parmesan cheese
¼ cup chopped pine nuts or blanched almonds
¼ cup chopped parsley

1 tablespoon chopped fresh basil or 1½ teaspoons dried basil
1 tablespoon lemon juice or white wine vinegar
¼ teaspoon black pepper

1. While eggs are boiling, prepare asparagus. Peel off outer skin of stems if necessary; otherwise snap off tough stem end and peel away large scales. Cut asparagus on the diagonal in 2-inch lengths. Cook in boiling salted water until just tender, about 3 to 5 minutes.
2. Rinse asparagus immediately under cold water to stop cooking. Drain well on paper towels. Cool eggs; peel and cut into fourths. Chill asparagus and eggs.
3. Make dressing in small bowl by beating yogurt, cheese, pine nuts, parsley, basil, lemon juice, lemon rind, and black pepper to combine.
4. Combine dressing and asparagus; place in serving bowl. Place quartered eggs over top in decorative pattern, sprinkling with more parsley if desired. Makes four servings.

Note for brown baggers: Place 1 cup asparagus with dressing in salad container; top with 4 egg quarters. Chill overnight.

You may substitute 2 10-ounce packages frozen asparagus spears for fresh asparagus.

Nutrition Note: For fat/cholesterol watchers, substitute 8 ounces cooked chicken, turkey, or skim-milk cheese for eggs.

HEARTY EGGPLANT SALAD

1 medium-size eggplant
 (about 1 pound)
2 medium-size tomatoes
½ cup chopped onion
½ cup chopped parsley
2 cloves garlic, crushed
½ teaspoon grated lemon rind
¼ teaspoon black pepper
2 to 3 tablespoons olive oil
1 tablespoon lemon juice
Paprika
2 cups diced cooked chicken
 (about ½ pound)

1. Preheat oven to 350°F. Place eggplant on baking sheet; bake 45 minutes or until very tender. Cut off stem end of eggplant; place open-end-down in a bowl for eggplant to drain.
2. When eggplant is cool, cut in half; scrape out pulp. Using a fork, mash pulp coarsely. Peel tomatoes, cut in half crosswise, chop coarsely, add to eggplant.
3. Stir in onion, parsley, garlic, lemon rind, and black pepper. Add olive oil, lemon juice, 1 teaspoon at a time, tasting for flavor.
4. Mound salad in center of serving platter, sprinkle with paprika, surround with diced chicken. Chill until serving time. Makes four servings.

Note for brown baggers: Place one-fourth of eggplant salad in a salad container. Top with one-fourth chicken cubes. Chill over-night.

LENTIL AND TOMATO SALAD

½ 16-ounce package dried
 lentils (about 1 cup)
1 cup finely sliced scallions
1 clove garlic, crushed
⅓ cup olive oil
2 tablespoons red wine vinegar
1 cup diced, cooked chicken
 or turkey, (about 4 ounces)
½ cup chopped parsley
½ teaspoon black pepper
4 large tomatoes

1. Cook lentils according to package directions, until just tender. Drain off any liquid and immediately stir in scallions, garlic, olive oil, and vinegar. Let lentils cool to room temperature.
2. Add chicken, parsley, and black pepper to lentil mixture. Toss to combine; set aside. Cut slice from top of tomatoes, about ¾ inch deep. Using a teaspoon, scoop out center of each tomato. Fill each tomato with lentil salad. Chill until serving time along with any extra salad. Makes four servings.

Note for brown baggers: Place filled tomato in a salad container. Chill overnight.

LIMA BEAN AND CHEESE SALAD

- 1 16-ounce poly-bag frozen baby lima beans
- 2 small zucchini, sliced (about 2 cups)
- 2 cups cubed feta cheese (about 8 ounces)
- 1 cup coarsely broken walnuts

Dressing

- ¾ cup low-fat, unflavored yogurt
- 2 tablespoons lemon juice
- 2 tablespoons chopped fresh dill weed or 1 tablespoon dried dill weed
- 1 teaspoon grated lemon rind
- ¼ teaspoon black pepper

Lettuce leaves

1. Cook baby lima beans according to package directions. Drain, cool, and chill. Gently stir in sliced zucchini, feta cheese, and walnuts. Return to refrigerator.
2. Make dressing by combining yogurt, lemon juice, dill, lemon rind, and black pepper. Chill until serving time.
3. Serve by mounding lima bean salad on lettuce-leaf lined platter. Serve dressing alongside.

Note for brown baggers: Place one-fourth lima bean-cheese salad in salad container; place one-fourth dressing in smaller, tight-seal container. Chill overnight. Pour dressing over salad just before eating.

Nutrition Note: Two-and-a-half cups fresh lima beans may be used, if in season, instead of frozen limas. And tofu (bean curd) may be used instead of feta cheese. Rinse feta cheese under cold water to remove brine, and pat dry on paper towels before using.

MACARONI, HAM AND CHEESE SALAD

- 1½ cups uncooked elbow macaroni
- ¼ cup low-fat, unflavored yogurt
- ¼ cup sour cream
- 2 tablespoons finely chopped onion
- 4 ounces Swiss cheese, cubed (about 1 cup)
- 2 tablespoons finely chopped green pepper
- 2 tablespoons chopped parsley
- 2 tablespoons prepared Dijon-style mustard
- 6 drops hot pepper sauce
- 4 ounces cooked ham, cubed (about 1 cup)

1. Cook macaroni according to package directions. Drain and let cool to room temperature. Place in large bowl. Add yogurt, sour cream, onion, green pepper, parsley, mustard, and hot pepper sauce. Toss well to blend.
2. Gently stir in cubed cheese and ham. Chill until serving time. Makes four servings.

Note for brown baggers: Place one-fourth salad in salad container. Chill overnight.

Nutrition Note: Skim-milk Mozzarella cheese may be substituted for Swiss cheese. Precooked turkey or chicken may be substituted for ham.

GERMAN-STYLE POTATO SALAD

Dressing

½ cup vegetable oil
¼ cup red wine vinegar

2 tablespoons prepared spicy mustard
¼ teaspoon black pepper

4 medium size potatoes (about 1½ pounds)
¼ cup chopped onion
1 clove garlic crushed
½ cup diced celery

½ cup diced green pepper
8 ounces cooked ham, diced (about 2 cups)
2 hard-cooked eggs, chopped
Chopped parsley (optional)

1. To make dressing: In a glass measuring cup beat together oil, vinegar, mustard, and black pepper. Let dressing stand at room temperature.
2. Peel potatoes; cut into ½-inch cubes. Cook in boiling, salted water until just tender, about 10 minutes. Drain well; stir in onion, garlic, and ¾ cup prepared dressing. Cool, then chill until serving time.
3. Place potato mixture in large salad bowl; gently toss in celery, green pepper, ham, and eggs. Sprinkle over remaining dressing; toss gently again. Sprinkle salad with parsley, if desired. Makes four servings.

Note for brown baggers: Place one-fourth salad in salad container. Chill overnight.

Nutrition Note: Twelve ounces (¾ pound) precooked chicken or turkey could be substituted for ham and eggs.

OLD-FASHIONED POTATO SALAD

4 medium-size potatoes (about 1½ pounds)
½ cup finely chopped celery
½ cup finely chopped green pepper
¼ cup chopped onion
¼ cup chopped dill pickle
¼ cup chopped parsley
8 ounces cooked ham or turkey in julienne strips (2 cups)

Dressing

¾ cup low-fat, unflavored yogurt or mayonnaise
1 tablespoon prepared spicy mustard
1 tablespoon lemon juice
1 teaspoon grated lemon rind
¼ teaspoon black pepper

1. Peel potatoes; cut into ¼-inch thick slices; cook in boiling, salted water until just tender, about 5 to 7 minutes. Drain and cool to room temperature.
2. Place potatoes in a large salad bowl. Gently toss with celery, green pepper, onion, dill pickle, and parsley. Stir in julienne ham strips.
3. In glass measuring cup beat together yogurt, mustard, lemon juice, lemon rind, and black pepper. Pour over salad; toss gently to combine. Chill until serving time. Makes four servings.

Note for brown baggers: Place one-fourth salad in salad container. Chill overnight.

POTATO AND TUNA SALAD

8 medium-size red-skinned potatoes (about 1 to 1¼ pounds)
½ pound fresh green beans, cut in 1-inch lengths (about 1½ cups)
2 hard-cooked eggs, shelled and quartered
1 7-ounce can water-packed tuna, drained
2 medium size tomatoes

Dressing

½ cup olive oil
¼ cup lemon juice or red wine vinegar
1 clove garlic, crushed
2 tablespoons chopped parsley
1 teaspoon grated lemon rind
¼ teaspoon black pepper

1. Cut potatoes into fourths; cook in boiling, salted water until tender, about 10 minutes. At same time in separate saucepans, cook green beans until tender, about 7 minutes, and hard cook eggs. Flake drained tuna and cut tomatoes into wedges.
2. Make dressing by combining olive oil, lemon juice, garlic, parsley, lemon rind, and black pepper. Drain potatoes and green beans. While still hot, sprinkle ¼ cup dressing over potatoes and 2 tablespoons dressing over green beans. Let cool to room temperature.
3. On an oblong serving platter make separate mounds of potatoes, green beans, quartered hard cooked eggs, tuna, and tomato wedges. Sprinkle remaining dressing over tuna and tomatoes. Chill until serving time. Makes four servings.

Note for brown baggers: Place one-fourth of all salad ingredients in a salad container. In a small tight-seal container place one-fourth of dressing. Chill overnight. Sprinkle salad dressing over salad just before eating.

Nutrition Note: Substitute 4 ounces cooked turkey, cut in strips (about 1 cup) for hard-cooked eggs.

RICE AND HAM SALAD

1 cup long-grain rice
¾ pound broccoli, broken in sprigs (about 2 cups)
1 small red onion, thinly sliced
2 medium-size tomatoes, cut in wedges
8 ounces pre-cooked ham, cut in ½-inch cubes (about 2 cups)

Dressing

¾ cup low-fat, unflavored yogurt or mayonnaise
2 tablespoons finely chopped parsley
2 tablespoons finely chopped basil or 2 teaspoons dried basil
2 tablespoons grated Parmesan cheese
1 teaspoon grated lemon rind
¼ teaspoon black pepper

1. Cook rice according to package directions. At same time, in separate saucepan in boiling water, cook broccoli sprigs until just

tender, about 5 to 7 minutes. Let rice and broccoli cool to room temperature.
2. In a large salad bowl combine rice, broccoli, red onion separated into rings, tomatoes, and ham.
3. Make dressing by beating together yogurt, parsley, basil, Parmesan cheese, lemon rind, and black pepper. Add to salad ingredients; toss gently to coat. Chill until serving time. Makes four servings.

Note for brown baggers: Place one-fourth salad in salad container. Chill overnight.

Nutrition Note: Eight ounces cooked chicken or turkey may be substituted for the ham.

CURRIED RICE AND TURKEY SALAD

2 tablespoons vegetable oil
¼ cup chopped onion
1 clove garlic, crushed
1 teaspoon curry powder
1 cup raw long-grain rice
2½ cups chicken broth or water
½ cup diced sweet red pepper
½ cup diced green pepper
½ cup chopped celery with leaves

8 ounces precooked turkey, cut in ½-inch cubes (about 2 cups)
¾ cup low-fat, unflavored yogurt or mayonnaise
2 tablespoons lemon juice
1 teaspoon grated lemon rind
¼ teaspoon black pepper

1. In medium saucepan heat oil; cook onion and garlic until tender. Sprinkle over curry powder; cook, stirring constantly, for 1 minute. Add rice; cook 1 minute longer.
2. Add chicken broth or water; simmer, covered, until rice is just tender, about 15 minutes. Let rice cool to room temperature. Stir in red pepper, green pepper, celery, and turkey.
3. In glass measuring cup beat together yogurt, lemon juice, lemon rind, and black pepper. Pour over salad. Stir gently to combine. Chill until serving time. Makes four servings.

Note for brown baggers: Place one-fourth salad in salad container. Chill overnight.

TOMATO MOZZARELLA SALAD

4 large tomatoes
1 8-ounce package skim-milk Mozzarella cheese, finely diced (about 2 cups)
1 cup finely shredded fresh spinach leaves
½ cup chopped fresh basil

Dressing

¼ cup olive oil
2 tablespoons lemon juice
1 teaspoon grated lemon rind
½ teaspoon black pepper

Lettuce leaves, optional

1. Peel tomatoes, if desired; cut in half crosswise and remove seeds. Dice tomato flesh, draining off any juice.
2. Toss tomato with Mozzarella cheese, spinach, and basil. Chill.
3. Make dressing by beating together olive oil, lemon juice, lemon rind, and black pepper. Just abefore serving toss dressing with salad ingredients. Serve on a bed of lettuce, if desired. Makes four servings.

Note for brown baggers: Place 1 cup tomato-Mozzarella mixture in a salad container. Place one-fourth of dressing in a smaller tight-seal container. Chill both overnight. Just before packing drain off any accumulated tomato juice from the salad. Sprinkle salad dressing over just before serving. Pack lettuce leaves separately.

TURKEY WALDORF SALAD

Dressing

¾ cup low-fat, unflavored yogurt or mayonnaise
1 tablespoon lemon juice
1 teaspoon grated lemon rind
6 drops hot pepper sauce

1 unpeeled red apple, diced (about 1 cup)
1 cup diced celery and leaves
1 cup green seedless grapes, halved
½ cup coarsely chopped walnuts
8 ounces cooked turkey, cubed (about 1 cup)
Romaine lettuce leaves (optional)

1. In a large bowl blend yogurt, lemon juice, lemon rind, and hot pepper sauce. Dice apple and immediately stir into dressing to prevent discoloring.
2. Stir in celery, grapes, and walnuts. Gently stir in turkey. Chill until serving time. Line large salad platter with Romaine lettuce leaves, if desired. Makes four servings.

Note for brown baggers: Place one-fourth salad in salad container. Chill overnight. Pack lettuce leaves separately.

6
SINGLE-SERVING SALADS

Every lunch box lover loves a salad. Crisp, cold, fresh ingredients are just what "eaten-out" salads often lack. Packing your own salad guarantees the best of seasonal vegetables. Just sprinkle with dressing at the last moment before eating. And for the busy person there is a selection of salad recipes to be prepared the night before.

All salads are designed for a single serving. They are the fresh, crisp, added touch needed to compliment a soup, stew, or cold, finger-lickin' food. These are vegetable salads, not main-dish salads. They range from tried-and-true lunch box favorites, such as carrot and celery sticks, to something more exotic for the adult brown bagger. Salads are an essential, healthful addition to any packed lunch.

NUTRITION KNOW-HOW:
- Here is a variety of salad recipes for a variety of palates. All contain the valuable element of fiber.
- Remember dark, green, leafy vegetables are a good source of vitamin A, and the cabbage family is always a good source of vitamin C.
- Deep yellow vegetables—carrots, pumpkin, sweet potato, and squash—are a good source of vitamin A. If you have leftover pumpkin or sweet potato, dice finely and substitute for carrots in one of our recipes—a good change of pace.
- Tomatoes—a firm salad favorite—have a high vitamin C content.
- Dressings are based on low-fat, unflavored yogurt or vegetable oil. Grated lemon rind is substituted for salt as a seasoning for the dressing.
- Fresh herbs are also used to flavor the salad and compensate for the ommission of salt.

Consumer Notes on Single-Serving Salads
- Vegetable salads are good crisp and cold. They are best packed in noncrushable boxes with tight-fitting lids. For the most part dressings are packed separately to be added at the last moment.
- For food-safety reasons it is unnecessary to pack salads in insulated containers. But do pack in an insulated lunch box so

salads remain crisp.
- You may want to pack yogurt- or mayonnaise-based salads in an insulated container. These are more vulnerable to spoilage.
- Discard any salad leftovers immediately on returning home.

ASPARAGUS SALAD

4 stalks fresh or 6 stalks frozen asparagus, slightly thawed
½ cup thinly sliced radishes

¼ cup slivered, toasted almonds

Dressing

2 tablespoons olive oil
1 tablespoon lemon juice

1 teaspoon prepared Dijon-style mustard

1. Cut asparagus into thin slices on the diagonal. Cook in a small saucepan in ¼ inch boiling water for 2 minutes or just until tender-crisp. Drain and cool completely.
2. Toss asparagus with radishes and toasted almonds. Place in salad container. Chill.
3. To make dressing: In smaller tight-seal container blend olive oil, lemon juice, and mustard. Sprinkle over salad just before eating. Makes one serving.

AVOCADO SALAD DIP WITH CUCUMBERS

1 small ripe avocado
1 small tomato, peeled and chopped
1 tablespoon finely chopped onion
½ clove garlic, crushed, optional

2 tablespoons lime or lemon juice
1 teaspoon grated lime or lemon rind
6 drops hot pepper sauce or to taste
1 small cucumber

1. Peel avocado and remove pit. Cut into chunks, then mash with fork. Peel tomato and chop; drain free of liquid and add to avocado.
2. Stir in chopped onion, garlic, lime juice, lime rind, and hot pepper sauce. Spoon ¾ cup avocado mixture into salad container.

(Reserve remainder for another use.) Press plastic wrap directly on surface of avocado mixture to prevent discoloring. Place lid on container; chill overnight.
3. Peel cucumber, cut in half lengthwise. Scoop out seeds with a teaspoon. Cut cucumber into sticks. Place in another salad container. Do not prepare cucumber sticks until last minute; they will wilt. Makes one serving.

GARBANZO BEAN SALAD

1 8-ounce can garbanzo beans, rinsed and drained
¼ cup chopped scallions
¼ cup chopped parsley
⅓ cup low-fat, unflavored yogurt
1 teaspoon grated lemon rind
⅛ teaspoon black pepper

1. In a salad container combine garbanzo beans, chopped scallions, and parsley. Stir in yogurt, lemon rind, and black pepper.
2. Chill overnight. Makes one serving.

THREE BEAN SALAD

½ cup frozen baby lima beans from 1 16-ounce poly-bag
½ cup frozen green beans, from 1 16-ounce poly-bag
1 8-ounce can red kidney beans, rinsed and drained

Dressing

3 tablespoons vegetable oil
1 tablespoon red wine vinegar
1 tablespoon finely chopped onion
½ clove garlic, crushed (optional)
⅛ teaspoon black pepper

1. In small saucepan in ¼ inch boiling water simmer lima beans 3 minutes. Add green beans; simmer, covered, 5 minutes longer. Drain; stir in red kidney beans.
2. To make dressing: In small measuring cup beat together vegetable oil, vinegar, chopped onion, garlic, and pepper. Pour over warm beans and toss to combine. Place in salad container; cool and chill overnight. Makes one serving.

Nutrition Note: Fresh limas and green beans can be used in season. Out-of-season use the frozen alternative.

BEAN AND PEPPER SLAW

½ cup finely shredded, fresh green beans
¼ cup very fine julienne strips green pepper
¼ cup very fine julienne strips sweet red pepper
¼ cup low-fat, unflavored yogurt or mayonnaise
¼ teaspoon celery seed
¼ teaspoon grated lemon rind
Black pepper

1. Toss green beans, green pepper and red pepper together. Stir in yogurt or mayonnaise, celery seed, lemon rind, and black pepper to taste.
2. Chill in salad container. This salad is good made one day and chilled overnight. Makes one serving.

Nutrition Note: Low-fat, unflavored yogurt is healthful but untraditional is a slaw. If you must use mayonnaise, look for a calorie-reduced one.

BEET AND ONION SALAD

1 8-ounce can julienne beets, drained
¼ cup thinly sliced onion rings
2 tablespoons vegetable oil
1 tablespoon red wine vinegar
½ teaspoon fennel seeds
½ teaspoon grated lemon rind
⅛ teaspoon black pepper

1. Gently toss together julienne beets and onion rings. Sprinkle over vegetable oil, vinegar, fennel seeds, lemon rind, and black pepper. Toss to combine.
2. Place in a salad container. Chill overnight. Makes one serving.

Note: Fresh beets can be used, but they require a long time to cook. If a small can is unavailable, measure a portion from a larger size.

CHINESE CABBAGE SLAW

½ cup finely shredded Chinese cabbage
½ cup finely shredded red cabbage
2 tablespoons sliced, pimiento-stuffed green olives
2 tablespoons chopped parsley
1 tablespoon capers, drained and chopped
¼ cup low-fat unflavored yogurt or mayonnaise

1. Toss together Chinese and red cabbage, sliced olives, chopped parsley, and capers. Gently fold in yogurt or mayonnaise.
2. Chill in salad container. This salad is good made overnight. Makes one serving.

CARROTS AND CELERY STICKS WITH A DIP

½ cup thin carrot sticks   ½ cup thin celery sticks

Dip for Vegetables

½ cup low-fat, unflavored yogurt
1 7½-ounce can minced clams, well drained
2 tablespoons chopped parsley
¾ teaspoon grated lemon rind
⅛ teaspoon black pepper

1. Place carrot and celery sticks in a salad container. Chill overnight.
2. To make dip: In a similar but insulated container combine yogurt, drained minced clams, parsley, lemon rind, and black pepper. Chill overnight. Use as a dip for carrots and celery or any vegetable. Makes one serving.

Note: For food-safety reasons, make sure the dip is packed in an insulated container.

CARROT AND ORANGE SALAD

1 medium carrot, peeled and grated (about ½ cup)
1 medium orange, peeled and cut into segments
¼ cup chopped parsley
2 tablespoons golden raisins
1 tablespoon olive or vegetable oil
2 teaspoons apple cider vinegar
⅛ teaspoon black pepper

1. Toss together grated carrot, orange segments, parsley, and golden raisins. Sprinkle with olive oil, vinegar, and pepper. Toss once more.
2. Chill in salad container. This salad is good made overnight. Makes one serving.

CAULIFLOWER BROCCOLI SALAD

½ cup tiny cauliflower sprigs
½ cup tiny broccoli sprigs
¼ cup chopped black olives
½ teaspoon grated lemon rind
⅛ teaspoon black pepper
2 tablespoons olive or vegetable oil
1 tablespoon lemon juice

1. In small saucepan in ¼ inch boiling water simmer cauliflower and broccoli until just tender, about 7 minutes. Drain and cool slightly.
2. While vegetables are still warm toss with black olives, lemon rind, and black pepper. Sprinkle with olive oil and lemon juice; toss again. Chill in salad container overnight. Makes one serving.

FENNEL SALAD

½ cup julienne strips fennel or celery
½ cup thin radish slices
½ teaspoon grated orange rind
¼ teaspoon fennel seeds (if celery is used)
½ teaspoon black pepper
2 tablespoons olive oil
1 tablespoon orange juice

1. Toss together fennel or celery strips, radishes, orange rind, fennel seeds (if necessary), and black pepper. Sprinkle with olive oil and orange juice. Toss again.
2. Chill in salad container. This salad is good made overnight. Makes one serving.

FRESH MIXED-VEGETABLE SALAD

1 small carrot, peeled and diced (about ½ cup)
½ cup fresh kernel corn
¼ cup fresh peas
¼ cup chopped celery leaves
½ teaspoon grated lemon rind
¼ teaspoon celery seed
⅛ teaspoon black pepper
½ cup low-fat unflavored yogurt or mayonnaise

1. In small saucepan in ¼ inch boiling water simmer carrots, kernel corn, and peas until just tender, about 5 minutes. Drain and cool completely.
2. Stir in celery leaves, lemon rind, celery seed, and black pepper. Gently fold in yogurt. Chill in salad container overnight. Makes one serving.

Note: Frozen kernel corn and peas from 1 16-ounce poly-bag may be used, if desired.

ORIENTAL VEGETABLE SALAD

1 cup fresh bean sprouts
½ cup thinly sliced water chestnuts
½ cup finely shredded snow peas or julienne strips celery
2 tablespoons chopped scallions

Ginger Peanut Dressing

2 tablespoons peanut oil
1 tablespoon lemon juice
1 tablespoon finely chopped, unsalted, dry roasted peanuts
½ teaspoon finely chopped ginger root or ½ teaspoon powdered ginger

1. Toss together bean sprouts, water chestnuts, snow peas, and scallions. Place in salad container. Chill.
2. To make dressing: In smaller tight-seal container blend peanut oil, lemon juice, chopped peanuts, and ginger. Chill. Sprinkle over salad just before eating. Makes one serving.

CORN PIMIENTO SALAD

1 small ear corn
2 roasted red peppers, from 1 7-ounce jar
2 tablespoons chopped scallions
2 tablespoons olive oil
1 tablespoon lime juice
½ teaspoon grated lime rind
⅛ teaspoon black pepper
4 to 6 drops hot pepper sauce

1. Cut kernels from corn ear; you should have about ¾ cup. In small saucepan in ¼ inch boiling water simmer kernel corn 3 to 5 minutes, or until tender. Drain.
2. Dice red peppers, discarding seeds and stems. Add to kernel corn along with chopped scallions. Sprinkle with olive oil, lime juice, lime rind, black pepper, and hot pepper sauce. Toss with corn-pepper mixture.
3. Place in salad container. Chill overnight. Makes one serving.

CRISP CUCUMBER SALAD

1 small, firm cucumber, peeled and thinly sliced (about ¾ cup)
1½ teaspoons salt
2 tablespoons olive oil
1 tablespoon white wine vinegar
1 tablespoon chopped, fresh dill weed or 1½ teaspoons dried dill weed
⅛ teaspoon black pepper

1. Place cucumbers in a glass or nonmetal pie plate. Sprinkle with salt. Cover and chill overnight.
2. Just before packing drain cucumbers, pressing out as much liquid as possible. Sprinkle with olive oil, vinegar, dill, and black pepper. Pack in salad container. Makes one serving.

Nutrition Note: Not a salad for sodium-conscious brown baggers.

DARK GREEN LEAFY SALAD WITH BUTTERMILK DRESSING

½ cup watercress sprigs
½ cup finely shredded fresh spinach leaves
½ cup finely shredded Romaine lettuce

Dressing

¼ cup buttermilk
1 teaspoon prepared Dijon-style mustard
¼ teaspoon grated lemon rind
⅛ teaspoon black pepper

1. Toss together watercress sprigs, shredded spinach, and Romaine lettuce. Place in salad container. Chill.
2. To make dressing: In a smaller tight-seal container mix buttermilk, mustard, lemon rind, and black pepper. Chill. Pour dressing over salad greens just before eating. Makes one serving.

MUSHROOM SALAD

¼ pound medium-size mushrooms, thinly sliced (about 1 cup)
1 tablespoon lemon juice
¼ cup finely chopped parsley

Dressing

2 tablespoons olive oil
1 tablespoon lemon juice
½ small clove garlic, crushed
¼ teaspoon grated lemon rind
Black pepper

1. Toss thinly sliced mushrooms with lemon juice to prevent discoloring; toss with chopped parsley. Place in salad container. Chill.
2. To make dressing: In smaller tight-seal container blend olive oil, lemon juice, crushed garlic, lemon rind, and black pepper to taste. Chill. Sprinkle dressing over salad just before eating. Makes one serving.

GREEN PEA AND LETTUCE SALAD

1 cup fresh or frozen green peas
½ cup finely shredded Iceberg lettuce
1 tablespoon thin julienne strips scallion

Dressing

2 tablespoons olive oil
1 tablespoon lemon juice or white wine vinegar
⅛ teaspoon black pepper
1½ teaspoons fresh snipped tarragon or dill weed or ¾ teaspoon dried tarragon or dill weed

1. In small saucepan in ¼ inch boiling water simmer peas until tender, about 5 minutes. Drain, cool, and chill completely.
2. Place peas in salad container together with shredded lettuce and scallions. Chill.
3. To make dressing: In smaller tight-seal container mix olive oil, lemon juice, snipped tarragon or dill weed, and black pepper. Chill. Pour dressing over salad just before eating. Makes one serving.

SQUASH SALAD

½ cup thinly sliced zucchini

½ cup thinly sliced summer squash

Dressing

2 tablespoons olive oil or vegetable oil
1 tablespoon lemon juice
1 tablespoon finely chopped walnuts or peanuts

1½ teaspoons snipped fresh dill weed or ¾ teaspoon dried dill weed
½ teaspoon grated lemon rind
⅛ teaspoon black pepper

1. Toss together zucchini and summer squash. Place in salad container. Chill.
2. To make dressing: In smaller tight-seal container mix olive oil, lemon juice, chopped nuts, dill weed, lemon rind, and black pepper. Chill. Pour dressing over salad vegetables just before eating. Makes one serving.

TOMATO SALAD

1 large ripe tomato, cut in wedges
2 tablespoons sliced black olives
2 tablespoons sliced green olives
1 tablespoon finely shredded fresh basil or 1½ teaspoons dried basil

1 tablespoon chopped parsley
½ teaspoon grated lemon rind
⅛ teaspoon black pepper
2 tablespoons olive oil or vegetable oil
1 tablespoon red wine vinegar or lemon juice

1. Toss together tomato wedges, sliced black and green olives, basil, parsley, lemon rind, and black pepper. Sprinkle with olive oil and red wine vinegar; toss again.
2. Place in salad container. Chill briefly but not overnight. Makes one serving.

7
QUICK MUFFINS AND BREADS

Quick muffins and breads are easy to make, easy to freeze, and a delicious and necessary addition to any lunch box. Delicious because they are a perfect accompaniment to soups, stews, and salads; necessary because they can be used to contain the essential makings of a salad and make a sandwich.

And because quick muffins and breads are slightly sweet, we recommend them as a substitute for snacks, desserts, and other traditional sweet treats—which should be programmed out of the nutritious brown bag lunch.

NUTRITION KNOW-HOW:
- Many people think bread is fattening, but breads are a chief source of energy for the body so they are especially important for school children.
- Without bread many other nutrients in the food we eat cannot be used by the body—another good reason why bread should be in the lunch box.
- Breads made with enriched flours, whole grains, grated vegetables, and nuts are rich in vitamin B, iron, and fiber.
- Make sure the all-purpose flour you use in baking is *enriched*.
- The recipes here incorporate whole-grain cereals, grated vegetables and chopped fresh fruits, dried fruits, and nuts—all nutrition and fiber boosters.
- The quantity of sugar in these recipes is less than in traditional recipes for making quick breads and muffins. Sweetness is a *learned* taste sensation. Train your family to like less sweet foods and appreciate the natural flavors of the other ingredients within the breads or muffins.
- Note that no salt is added to these breads. There is sufficient sodium (a principle constituent of salt) in baking powder and baking soda, which are the rising agents in these breads.
- If you are on a sodium-restricted diet, these breads are not for you. Pick the yeast-raised breads in Chapter 2. Above all, consult your physician as to what your diet allows.
- Muffins and breads containing cheese are not replacements for a

main-meal serving of protein. They do boost the protein content of the lunch box, and you can afford to have *slightly* less meat, fish, or eggs in other menu items.

Consumer Notes on Quick Muffins and Breads

Any baked muffin or bread needs a little extra care in order to guarantee the perfect end result. Before you begin baking, check the following:

- Make sure the oven temperature is accurate. Do not rely only on the oven thermostat; have an independent oven thermometer hanging from the top shelf so it is in the center of the oven. Accurate baking temperatures are essential.
- Measure all ingredients accurately. Dry ingredients must be measured in aluminum measuring cups and liquid ingredients in glass pyrex measures.
- Make sure baking pans are the correct size and are metal. Glass ovenware cooks more quickly than metal. If you use it, lower the oven temperature 25°.
- If muffin batter does not fill all muffin holes, fill empty ones with cold water before baking.
- Make sure oven shelves are placed accurately in the oven before heating. Muffins are best baked on a shelf one-third from the top of the oven. Breads are best baked on a shelf in the exact center of the oven.
- Muffins must be removed from the pan *immediately* after baking. Breads must sit in the pan, *on a wire rack,* for 5 to 10 minutes; then be turned out to cool completely on a wire rack. Also, you cannot slice a warm loaf as it will crumble.
- Muffins and breads, once cooled, should be wrapped in foil and refrigerated. If airtight, they will keep 3 to 4 days.
- Muffins and breads freeze well. Wrap as above, label, and freeze up to 6 months.

Note: Thaw large muffins in the refrigerator overnight before packing. *Pack muffins safely* in the lunch box by placing them in a separate container that cannot be crushed. Small muffins will thaw out in a lunch box between breakfast and lunch. If not eaten, do not be tempted to keep muffins and breads for the next day.

BANANA PEANUTTY BREAD

¾ cup light brown sugar, firmly packed
½ cup margarine
2 eggs
1 cup mashed banana (about 2 ripe medium bananas)
½ cup finely chopped, dry-roasted, unsalted peanuts

1 tablespoon grated lemon rind
2 cups all-purpose flour
2 teaspoons baking powder
½ teaspoon baking soda
¼ to ⅓ cup milk or low-fat milk

1. Preheat oven to 350°F. Grease and flour a 9 × 5 × 3-inch loaf pan.
2. In a large bowl with mixer at medium speed, beat sugar and margarine together. Add eggs. Beat until mixture is thick and creamy. At low speed stir in mashed banana, chopped peanuts, and lemon rind.
3. In medium bowl combine flour, baking powder, and baking soda. At low speed alternately fold dry ingredients and milk, into banana mixture. The batter should have a soft "dropping" consistency. Spoon batter into prepared pan.
4. Bake 60 to 70 minutes or until wooden toothpick or cake tester inserted in center comes out clean. Cool only 5 minutes in pan on wire rack. Remove from pan. Cool completely. Makes one 9 × 5 × 3-inch loaf.

APPLE NUT BREAD

½ cup margarine
½ cup light brown sugar, firmly packed
2 eggs
1 cup apple, peeled and coarsley chopped
½ cup chopped walnuts
½ cup golden raisins, coarsely chopped

2 cups all-purpose flour
1½ teaspoons baking powder
1 teaspoon cinnamon
½ teaspoon ginger
½ teaspoon baking soda
¼ to ⅓ cup milk or low-fat milk

1. Preheat oven to 350° F. Heavily grease and flour a 9 × 5 × 3-inch loaf pan.
2. In large bowl with mixer at medium speed, beat margarine and sugar together. Add eggs. Beat until mixture is thick and creamy. At low speed stir in chopped apples, raisins, and walnuts.
3. In a medium bowl combine flour, baking powder, cinnamon, ginger, and baking soda. At low speed alternately fold dry ingredients and milk into apple mixture. The batter should have soft "dropping" consistency. Spoon batter into prepared pan.
4. Bake 60 minutes or until wooden toothpick or cake tester inserted in center comes out clean. Cool in pan on wire rack 10 minutes. Remove from pan. Cool completely. Makes one 9 × 5 × 3-inch loaf.

CARROT BREAD

½ cup margarine
½ cup sugar
2 eggs
1 cup finely grated carrots, firmly packed
2 cups all-purpose flour
2 teaspoons baking powder

1 teaspoon cinnamon
½ teaspoon baking soda
½ cup milk or low-fat milk
1 tablespoon lemon juice
1 teaspoon vanilla extract

1. Preheat oven to 350°F. Grease and flour a 9 × 5 × 3-inch loaf pan.
2. In large bowl with mixer at medium speed, beat margarine and sugar together. Add eggs. Beat until mixture is thick and creamy. At low speed stir in grated carrots.
3. In medium bowl combine flour, baking powder, cinnamon, and baking soda. In measuring cup beat together milk, lemon juice, and vanilla extract.
4. At low speed alternately fold dry ingredients and milk mixture into carrot mixture. Spoon batter into prepared pan. Bake 60 minutes or until wooden toothpick or cake tester inserted in center comes out clean. Cool in pan on wire rack 10 minutes. Remove from pan. Cool completely. Makes one 9 × 5 × 3-inch loaf.

CRANBERRY HARVEST LOAF

2 cups all-purpose flour
¾ cup brown sugar, firmly packed
1 tablespoon grated orange rind
1½ teaspoons baking powder
½ teaspoon baking soda
¾ cup orange juice
¼ cup margarine, melted
1 egg
1 cup fresh or frozen cranberries, coarsely chopped
¾ chopped walnuts

1. Preheat oven to 350°F. Grease and flour a 9 × 5 × 3-inch loaf pan.
2. In large bowl combine flour, brown sugar, orange rind, baking powder, and baking soda. In a 2-cup measure beat together orange juice, melted margarine, and egg.
3. Beat juice mixture into dry ingredients, stirring until just combined. Gently fold in chopped cranberries and nuts.
4. Spoon batter into prepared pan. Bake 60 minutes or until wooden toothpick or cake tester comes out clean. Cool in pan on wire rack 10 minutes. Remove from pan. Cool completely. Makes one 9 × 5 × 3-inch loaf.

CHILI CHEESE SKILLET BREAD

1 cup all-purpose flour
1 cup yellow cornmeal
4 teaspoons baking powder
½ to 1 teaspoon chili powder
1 cup grated sharp Cheddar cheese
½ cup finely grated onion
1 cup milk or low-fat milk
1 egg

1. Preheat oven to 425°F. Grease an 8-inch ovenproof skillet or 8-inch square baking pan.
2. In large bowl combine flour, cornmeal, baking powder, and chili powder. Stir in cheese and onion. In 2-cup measure beat together milk and egg. Stir into dry ingredients until just combined.
3. Spoon batter into prepared skillet or pan. Bake 25 to 30 minutes or until wooden toothpick or cake tester comes out clean. Cook completely in skillet or pan. Cut into wedges to serve. Makes one square 8-inch bread.

DILLY POTATO BREAD

1 cup all-purpose flour
½ cup whole-wheat flour
½ cup fresh (not instant) mashed potatoes
2 tablespoons chopped fresh dill or 1 tablespoon dried dill weed
1½ teaspoons caraway seed (optional)
½ cup small-curd low-fat cottage cheese
1 egg
¾ cup milk or low-fat milk

1. Preheat oven to 400°F. Heavily grease an 8-inch square baking pan.
2. In large bowl combine all-purpose and whole-wheat flour. Using 2 knives or a pastry cutter, cut in mashed potatoes until mixture resembles coarse cornmeal. Stir in dill and caraway seeds, if desired.
3. In 2-cup measure beat together cheese, egg, and milk. Stir into flour mixture just to moisten dry ingredients. Spoon butter into prepared pan. Bake 25 to 30 minutes or until wooden toothpick or cake tester inserted in center comes out clean. Cool completely in pan on wire rack. Cut into 2-inch squares to serve. Makes 16 servings or one square 8-inch bread.

ONION PEPPER BREAD

¼ cup vegetable oil
1 cup chopped onion
2 cloves garlic, finely chopped
1 teaspoon to 1 tablespoon chopped green jalapeño peppers
¼ teaspoon black pepper or hot pepper sauce (optional)
¾ cup milk or low-fat milk
1 egg
1½ cups all-purpose flour
½ cup yellow cornmeal

1. Preheat oven to 400°F. Heavily grease an 8-inch square baking pan.
2. In medium skillet over medium heat heat oil. Add onion and garlic. Cook until onion is golden brown, about 7 to 10 minutes.
3. Stir in jalapeño pepper to taste, and black pepper or hot pepper sauce, if desired. Slowly beat in milk and then egg.
4. In large mixing bowl combine all-purpose flour and cornmeal. Stir liquids into flour mixture just to moisten. Spoon batter into prepared pan. Bake 30 minutes or until wooden toothpick or cake tester, inserted in center, comes out clean. Cool completely

in pan on wire rack. Cut into 2-inch squares to serve. Makes 16 servings or one square 8-inch bread.

PUMPKIN RAISIN BREAD

¾ to 1 cup sugar
⅓ cup margarine
2 eggs
1 cup mashed, cooked pumpkin
1½ cups all-purpose flour
1 teaspoon baking powder
1 teaspoon cinnamon
½ teaspoon nutmeg
½ teaspoon allspice
½ teaspoon baking soda
⅓ to ½ cup milk or low-fat milk
½ cup golden raisins, coarsely chopped
½ cup chopped walnuts

1. Preheat oven to 350°F. Grease and flour a 9 × 5 × 3-inch loaf pan.
2. In large bowl with electric mixer at medium speed, beat sugar and margarine together. Add eggs and beat until mixture is thick and creamy. Beat in pumpkin.
3. In a medium bowl mix together flour, baking powder, cinnamon, nutmeg, allspice, and baking soda. At low speed alternately add flour mixture and milk to pumpkin mixture. Batter should have a soft "dropping" consistency. Fold in raisins and walnuts.
4. Spoon batter into prepared pan. Bake 50 to 60 minutes or until wooden toothpick or cake tester inserted in center comes out clean. Cool in pan on wire rack 10 minutes. Remove from pan. Cool completely. Makes one 9 × 5 × 3-inch loaf.

WHOLE-WHEAT ZUCCHINI BREAD

1 cup all-purpose flour
1 cup whole-wheat flour
½ cup sugar
1½ teaspoon baking powder
1 teaspoon grated lemon rind
½ teaspoon baking soda
1 cup grated zucchini, firmly packed and pressed dry
½ cup finely chopped walnuts or pecans
¾ cup buttermilk
¼ cup vegetable oil
2 eggs

1. Preheat oven to 350°F. Grease and flour a 9 × 5 × 3-inch loaf pan.

2. In a large bowl, combine all-purpose flour, whole-wheat flour, sugar, baking powder, lemon rind, and baking soda.
3. Stir in zucchini and walnuts. In 2-cup measure beat together buttermilk, vegetable oil, and eggs. Stir into flour mixture just to moisten dry ingredients.
4. Spoon batter into prepared pan. Bake 50 to 60 minutes or until wooden toothpick or cake tester comes out clean. Cool in pan on wire rack 10 minutes. Remove from pan. Cool completely. Makes one 9 × 5 × 3-inch loaf.

OATMEAL SODA BREAD

3 cups all-purpose flour
1 cup quick-cooking oats
1 cup currants or dark raisins, coarsely chopped
2 teaspoons baking powder

1 teaspoon baking soda
2 eggs, beaten
1¼ to 1½ cups buttermilk

1. Preheat oven to 350°F. In large bowl combine flour, oats, currants, baking powder, and baking soda. Make a well in center of dry ingredients.
2. Add eggs and sufficient buttermilk to make a soft but kneadable dough.
3. Turn dough onto floured surface and knead lightly, turning 6 to 8 times.
4. Shape into 8-inch round. Place on lightly floured (not greased) cookie sheet. Cut cross on top, spreading open slightly. Bake 45 to 50 minutes or until loaf is lightly browned and sounds hollow when tapped. Cool completely on wire rack. Makes one round 8-inch loaf.

BACON CORNMEAL MUFFINS

4 to 6 slices bacon
1 cup all-purpose flour
1 cup yellow cornmeal
4 teaspoons baking powder
½ to 1 teaspoon cracked black pepper

¼ cup bacon fat or vegetable oil
1 egg
1 cup milk or low-fat milk

1. In medium skillet fry bacon slices until crisp. Place on paper towels to drain. Crumble to measure ½ cup and set aside. Reserve bacon fat.
2. Preheat oven to 425°F. Heavily grease a 12-hole (each 2½ × 1-inch) muffin pan, or line each muffin hole with paper baking liners.
3. In large bowl combine all-purpose flour, cornmeal, baking powder, and black pepper to taste. Stir in crumbled bacon. Make a well in center of mixture.
4. Measure ¼ cup reserved bacon fat, adding vegetable oil if necessary to make up volume. Beat in egg. Add to center of dry ingredients. Add milk and quickly stir with a fork to blend ingredients until moist.
5. Fill each muffin hole three-fourths full of batter. Bake 15 to 20 minutes or until toothpick or cake tester inserted in center of muffin comes out clean. Remove muffins from pans immediately to wire rack to cool. Makes 12 muffins.

Nutrition Note: With bacon and bacon fat being two prime ingredients, these muffins are an occasional treat only and definitely not for the 100 percent nutrition-conscious person.

Peanut Cornmeal Muffins. A more healthful muffin can be made by substituting ½ cup chopped, unsalted, dry-roasted peanuts and vegetable oil for the bacon fat. This will give a savory muffin. For a sweet version, omit the pepper and substitute 2 to 4 tablespoons sugar to taste.

DATE MUFFINS

1 cup whole-wheat flour
1 cup all-purpose flour
½ cup finely chopped dates
¼ cup brown sugar, firmly packed
4 teaspoons baking powder
¼ cup margarine, melted, or vegetable oil
1 egg
1 cup milk or low-fat milk

1. Preheat oven to 425°F. Heavily grease a 12-hole (each 2½ × 1-inch) muffin pan, or line each muffin hole with paper baking liner.
2. In large bowl combine whole-wheat flour, all-purpose flour, dates, brown sugar, and baking powder. Stir to mix well. Make a well in center of mixture.

3. In a measuring cup beat together melted margarine and egg. Add to center of dry ingredients. Add milk and quickly stir with a fork to blend ingredients until moist.
4. Fill each muffin hole three-fourths full of batter. Bake 15 to 20 minutes or until toothpick or cake tester inserted in center of muffin comes out clean. Remove muffins from pan immediately to wire rack to cool. Makes 12 muffins.

ORANGE RAISIN MUFFINS

1 cup all-purpose flour
½ cup whole-wheat flour
½ cup wheat germ
½ cup golden raisins, coarsely chopped
¼ cup sugar
4 teaspoons baking powder

1 tablespoon grated orange rind
¼ cup orange juice
¼ cup margarine, melted, or vegetable oil
1 egg
¾ cup milk or low-fat milk

1. Preheat oven to 425°F. Heavily grease a 12-hole (each 2½ × 1-inch) muffin pan, or line each muffin hole with paper baking liner.
2. In large bowl combine all-purpose flour, whole-wheat flour, wheat germ, raisins, sugar, baking powder, and orange rind. Make a well in center of mixture.
3. In a measuring cup beat together orange juice, melted margarine, and egg. Add to center of dry ingredients. Add milk and quickly stir with a fork to blend ingredients until moist.
4. Fill each muffin hole three-fourths full of batter. Bake 15 to 20 minutes or until toothpick or cake tester inserted in center of muffin comes out clean. Remove muffins from pan immediately to wire rack to cool. Makes 12 muffins.

TOASTED-WHEAT BUTTERMILK MUFFINS

1 cup toasted-wheat, ready-to-cook cereal
1 cup buttermilk
¼ cup margarine, melted, or vegetable oil

1 egg
1 cup all-purpose flour
¼ cup sugar
3 tablespoons sesame seeds
4 teaspoons baking powder

1. In large bowl blend toasted-wheat cereal, buttermilk, melted margarine, and egg. Beat well to mix. Let stand 10 minutes.
2. Preheat oven to 425°F. Heavily grease a 12-hole (each 2½ × 1-inch) muffin pan, or line each muffin hole with paper baking liner.
3. In small bowl blend together all-purpose flour, sugar, 2 tablespoons sesame seeds, baking powder, and baking soda. Stir mixture quickly into moistened wheat cereal mixture, stirring just to combine.
4. Fill each muffin hole three-fourths full of batter. Sprinkle top of each muffin with a little of remaining 1 tablespoon sesame seeds. Bake 15 to 20 minutes or until toothpick or cake tester inserted in center of muffin comes out clean. Remove muffins from pan immediately to wire rack to cool. Makes 12 muffins.

WALNUT BRAN MUFFINS

1 cup bran cereal
1 cup milk or low-fat milk
¼ cup vegetable oil
1 egg
1 cup all-purpose flour
½ cup chopped walnuts
¼ cup sugar
4 teaspoons baking powder

1. In large bowl blend bran cereal, milk, vegetable oil, and egg. Beat well to mix. Let stand 10 minutes.
2. Preheat oven to 425°F. Heavily grease a 12-hole (each 2½ × 1-inch) muffin pan, or line each muffin hole with paper baking liner.
3. In small bowl blend together all-purpose flour, walnuts, sugar, and baking powder. Stir mixture quickly into moistened bran, stirring just to combine.
4. Fill each muffin hole three-fourths full of batter. Bake 15 to 20 minutes, or until toothpick or cake tester inserted in center of muffin comes out clean. Remove muffins from pan immediately to wire rack to cool. Makes 12 muffins.

STUFFIN' MUFFINS

1 cup corn-bread stuffing mix
or herbed stuffing mix,
coarsely crushed
1 cup milk or low-fat milk

1 egg
1 cup all-purpose flour
4 teaspoons baking powder

1. In large bowl place crushed stuffing mix. In small saucepan heat milk and oil until summering around edge of pan. Beat into stuffing mix. Let stand 10 minutes.
2. Preheat oven to 425°F. Heavily grease a 12-hole (each 2½ × 1-inch) muffin pan, or line each muffin hole with paper baking liner.
3. Beat egg into cooled stuffing mix. Combine flour and baking powder and stir into stuffing mixture just until blended.
4. Fill each muffin hole three-fourths full of batter. Bake 15 to 20 minutes or until toothpick or cake tester inserted in center of muffin comes out clean. Remove muffins from pan immediately to wire rack to cool. Makes 12 muffins.

Note: A savory muffin that goes well with cold chicken or turkey.

SAVORY CHEESE BISCUITS

1¼ cups all-purpose flour
¾ cup yellow cornmeal
4 teaspoons baking powder
¼ teaspoon hot paprika or
cayenne pepper

½ cup margarine
½ cup grated sharp Cheddar cheese
⅔ cup milk or low-fat milk

1. Preheat oven to 450°F. In large bowl combine all-purpose flour, cornmeal, baking powder, and pepper.
2. Using two knives or a pastry cutter, cut in margarine until mixture resembles coarse cornmeal. Stir in grated cheese. Add milk and mix quickly with a fork just so dough comes together.
3. Turn onto lightly-floured surface and knead gently for 30 seconds. Pat or roll dough into ¾-inch thick circle. Using 2½-inch cutter, cut dough into biscuits.
4. Place on ungreased cookie sheet, spacing evenly. Bake 12 to 15 minutes or until risen and golden brown. Makes 10 to 12 servings.

Nutrition Note: Any firm skim-milk cheese may be substituted for the Cheddar cheese used here.

HERBED BISCUITS

1 cup all-purpose flour
1 cup whole-wheat flour
4 teaspoons baking powder
½ cup margarine

2 tablespoons chopped fresh parsley, dill or basil
⅔ cup milk or low-fat milk

1. Preheat oven to 450°F. In large bowl combine all-purpose flour, whole-wheat flour and baking powder.
2. Using two knives or pastry cutter, cut in margarine until mixture resembles coarse cornmeal. Stir in one chopped fresh herb. Add milk and mix quickly with fork just so dough comes together.
3. Turn onto lightly-floured surface and knead gently for 30 seconds. Pat or roll dough into ¾-inch thick circle. Using 2½-inch cutter, cut dough into biscuits.
4. Place on ungreased cookie sheet, spacing evenly. Bake 12 to 15 minutes or until risen and golden brown. Makes 10 to 12 biscuits.

Note: 2 teaspoons dried dill or basil may be substituted for the fresh herbs. Dried parsley is not recommended.

OATMEAL BISCUITS

1 cup quick-cooking oatmeal
1 cup all-purpose flour
4 teaspoons baking powder

¼ teaspoon black pepper
½ cup margarine
⅔ cup milk or low-fat milk

1. Preheat oven to 450°F. In small heavy skillet over low heat, toast oats until pale golden, shaking pan or stirring constantly, about 5 minutes. Pour at once into small bowl to cool.
2. In large bowl combine flour, baking powder, and pepper. Using two knives or pastry cutter, cut in margarine until mixture resembles coarse cornmeal. Add cooled, toasted oatmeal. Add milk and mix quickly with fork just until dough comes together.
3. Turn onto lightly flavored surface and knead gently for 30 seconds. Pat or roll dough into ¾-inch thick circle. Using 2½-inch cutter, cut dough into biscuits.
4. Place on ungreased cookie sheet, spacing evenly. Bake 12 to 15 minutes or until risen and golden brown. Makes 10 to 12 biscuits.

WHOLE-WHEAT BLUEBERRY BISCUITS

1 cup all-purpose flour
1 cup whole-wheat flour
4 teaspoons baking powder
2 tablespoons sugar
1 teaspoon grated orange rind

½ cup margarine
½ cup fresh or dry, frozen blueberries
⅔ cup milk or low-fat milk

1. Preheat oven to 450°F. In large bowl combine all-purpose flour, whole-wheat flour, baking powder, sugar, and orange rind.
2. Using two knives or a pastry cutter, cut in margarine until mixture resembles coarse cornmeal. Stir in blueberries. Add milk and mix quickly with fork just so dough comes together.
3. Turn onto lightly-floured surface and knead gently for 30 seconds. Pat or roll dough into ¾-inch thick circle. Using 2½-inch cutter, cut dough into biscuits.
4. Place on ungreased cookie sheet, spacing evenly. Bake 12 to 15 minutes or until risen and golden brown. Makes 10 to 12 biscuits.

8
LIGHT FRUIT DESSERTS

The traditional lunch box dessert—a piece of chilled fresh fruit added just before closing the lid—is a dessert that can't be beat. It is simple, easy to prepare, and, if you choose the right fruit, packed full of fiber, vitamins, minerals, and its own natural sugar.

But when you're looking to add something special to a lunch box, nothing says you care more than adding a special, slightly-sweet treat. While hard to make in single portion sizes, here's an easy solution for having them on hand: Make a light dessert for dinner, and pack a portion for your brown bag luncher at the same time. All the desserts in this chapter are planned to hold in the refrigerator overnight. Provided they are packed in an *insulated* container, they will travel perfectly to school, the office, or work the next day.

NUTRITION KNOW-HOW:
- Fruits are rich in vitamins. It is most important to know that oranges, stawberries, grapefruit, and lemons are rich in vitamin C, as is pineapple to a lesser extent.
- Deep yellow-red fruits are rich in vitamin A. Pick from among apricots, cantalopes, nectarines, peaches, pumpkin, and watermelon. Blueberries, cherries, and plums have lesser amounts, but cannot be ignored.
- All fruits are an excellent source of fiber and minerals.
- All fruits have natural sugar. As you make a recipe, taste the fruit for sweetness and add additional sugar to taste—if at all. Above all, gradually train your palate to like foods that are less sweet. Tangy desserts are more refreshing.
- Make fruit desserts light and fluffy by folding in beaten egg-whites. They are low in calories, and an aerated dessert is cool and easy to eat. The big volume tricks the eye into believing there is more to eat than there really is.
- Use of dried fruits, with their concentrated natural sugar, eliminates the need to add more sweetness to the dish.
- Where possible, use low-fat, unflavored yogurt instead of heavy cream. Desserts that use heavy cream really are a *sometime* treat, as are those using egg yolks.

Consumer Notes on Light Fruit Desserts

- Although light fruit desserts are easy and simple to make, the "trick" is to remember to keep the proportions of the recipes in which gelatin is used very accurate. One envelope of unflavored gelatin sets 2 cups of liquid; but if the liquid is acid, the setting properties will be weakened. Egg whites are not part of this volume.
- Dissolving gelatin needs care: sprinkle over liquid to soften and then heat to melt. Add only warm gelatin to warm liquid. Hot gelatin in a cold liquid will cause stringy "ribbons" to form.
- For maximum volume on egg whites, make sure they are free of yolks and at room temperature before beating.
- Pack all desserts in a firm container with a tight-seal lid.

Pack desserts *safely* by keeping chilled at all times and carrying in an *insulated* lunch box or container. Any desserts not eaten *must be* discarded.

NEW-STYLE AMBROSIA

4 large, seedless oranges
2 20-ounce cans pineapple rings in natural juice
2 tablespoons honey (optional)
½ cup toasted, slivered almonds, pine nuts or sesame seeds

1. Using small sharp knife, cut peel from orange to remove both rind and pith. Cut oranges in slices crosswise. Over glass measuring cup, squeeze rind to remove any juice.
2. Drain pineapple juice into measuring cup. Arrange pineapple rings alternately with orange slices on large shallow platter. Drizzle with honey if desired. Spoon a little reserved juice over fruit slices just to moisten. Chill. Sprinkle with nuts or sesame seeds just before serving. Makes four servings.

Note for brown baggers: Place one-forth orange slices and pineapple rings in salad container with tight-seal lid. Separately pack nuts or sesame seeds and sprinkle over fruit just before eating.

Nutrition Note: Ambrosia traditionally is sprinkled with toasted coconut. Since this ingredient contains saturated fat, we suggest more healthful alternates.

BAKED STUFFED APPLES

4 large, tart, green baking apples (Granny Smith preferred)

Filling

¼ cup chopped dark raisins
¼ cup finely snipped dates
1 teaspoon powdered cinnamon
4 teaspoons margarine

Water

1. Preheat oven to 350°F. Wash and dry apples. Using a potato peeler, cut band of peel from the middle circumference of each apple and, using apple corer, remove core from each apple.
2. Make filling in small bowl by mixing raisins, dates, and cinnamon to combine. Place apples in lightly greased 8-inch square baking dish. Fill center of each with dried fruit mixture. Top each with 1 teaspoon margarine. Pour water to depth of ¼ inch around apples.
3. Bake for 35 to 45 minutes until apples are tender but not collapsed. Add more water during cooking process if baking dish looks dry. Serve warm or chilled. Makes four servings.

Note for brown baggers: Using broad spatula, lift apple from dish to a deep firm container with tight-seal lid. Chill overnight.

Nutrition Note: Dried fruit contains sufficient natural sugar to sweeten the apples. If you have a sweet tooth, do any or all of the following:
- Substitute a sweet dessert apple such as Golden Delicious for the tart baking apple.
- Add between 1 to 2 tablespoons sugar to the filling before stuffing the apples.

APPLE APRICOT MEDLEY

2 large, tart, green apples (preferably Granny Smith)
1 cup dried apricot halves (about 30 halves)
½ cup water
¼ cup orange juice
¼ cup lemon juice
1 teaspoon almond extract
Brown sugar to taste (optional)
½ cup toasted, slivered almonds

1. Core and slice apples into wedges approximately ⅓-inch thick. In a medium saucepan combine apples with apricot halves.
2. Add water, orange and lemon juice, and almond extract to saucepan. Simmer apples and apricots, covered, for 5 minutes.
3. Remove from heat. Cover and let stand for 5 minutes. Taste for sweetness. Stir in brown sugar to taste, if necessary. Place in serving bowl. Chill until serving time. Sprinkle with almonds. Makes four servings.

Note for Brown Baggers: Place ¾ cup in tight-seal container. Chill overnight. Sprinkle with 2 tablespoons almonds just before eating. Or you can stir almonds in just before chilling—less crunchy but still delicious.

APPLE FOOL

2 sweet baking apples (preferably Rome Beauty)
1 envelope unflavored gelatin
½ cup orange juice
2 teaspoons grated orange rind
2 egg whites
2 to 4 tablespoons sugar

1. Preheat oven to 350°F. Wash and dry apples. Using potato peeler, cut a band of peel from middle circumference of each apple and, using apple corer, remove core from each apple.
2. Place apples in small baking dish. Add water to a depth of ¼ inch. Bake 35 to 45 minutes or until tender. Meanwhile, in small custard cup sprinkle gelatin over orange juice. Let stand to soften. Place cup in small skillet or saucepan of water. Heat to dissolve gelatin.
3. Cool apples slightly. Using a mixer or food processor, beat tender apple flesh to pureé. This should measure approximately 2 cups. While pureé is still warm, stir in dissolved gelatin and orange rind. Cool and chill until semiset.
4. In medium bowl with mixer at high speed, beat egg whites until soft peaks form. Slowly beat in sugar until stiff peaks form. Quantity of sugar added will depend on sweetness of apple pureé. Fold egg whites into apple pureé. Divide dessert between four 10-ounce dessert dishes. Makes four servings.

Note for Brown Baggers: Make one dessert directly in firm container with tight-seal lid. Chill overnight. Pack in insulated lunch box.

APRICOTS IN ORANGE SAUCE

1½ to 2 pounds fresh ripe apricots (about 16 to 20 apricots)

Filling

1 cup chopped dates or golden raisins
1 8-ounce can blanched almonds, finely chopped
1 egg white
1 teaspoon almond extract

Sauce

½ cup orange marmalade
½ cup orange juice

1. Wash and dry apricots. Using tip of sharp knife, cut around center of each apricot, making slit just sufficient to remove pit.
2. Preheat oven to 350°F. To make filling: In small bowl mix together dates and almonds. In a small custard cup blend together egg white and almond extract. Add egg white mixture, a little at a time, to dried fruit, pressing with a fork to make a soft dough.
3. Using heaping teaspoon of filling, roll into ball and place inside apricot. Use to fill all apricots. Place apricots in lightly greased 8-inch square baking dish.
4. To make sauce: Beat together orange marmalade and orange juice. Pour over apricots. Bake, uncovered, 20 to 25 minutes or until apricots are tender but not mushy. Serve hot or cold. Makes four servings.

Note for Brown Baggers: Place 4 or 5 stuffed apricots and a little sauce in firm container with tight-seal lid. Chill overnight.

Nutrition Note: To minimize sugar content of this dish, substitute more orange juice for orange marmalade.

BANANA PUDDING

¼ to ⅓ cup sugar
¼ cup cornstarch
2 cups milk or low-fat milk
1 teaspoon vanilla extract
2 eggs, separated
1 medium-size, just-ripe banana, thinly sliced
½ cup vanilla wafers, crushed, (about 10 wafers)

1. In medium saucepan blend cornstarch and sugar to taste. Slowly stir in milk, keeping mixture smooth. Bring to boiling point over medium heat, stirring constantly to keep smooth.
2. Remove from heat. Cool 1 minute, stirring constantly. Beat in vanilla extract and egg yolks. Gently fold in sliced banana. Cool to room temperature, covering with plastic wrap to prevent skin forming.
3. Sprinkle 2 tablespoons vanilla wafer crumbs over bottom of four 10-ounce dessert dishes. In small bowl with mixer at high speed, beat egg whites until stiff. Fold into pudding mixture. Divide pudding between dessert dishes. Chill at least 1 hour. Makes four servings.

Note for Brown Baggers: Make one dessert directly in a firm container with tight-seal lid. Chill overnight. Pack in insulated lunch box.
Nutrition Note: Cholesterol watchers may want to avoid egg yolk. However, do use the egg whites to lighten the pudding.

VERY BERRY SALAD

1 pint strawberries, washed, hulled and sliced
1 pint blueberries, washed
1 cup orange juice
¼ cup honey
2 2-inch strips orange peel
½ teaspoon almond extract

1. Place prepared strawberries and blueberries in a serving bowl.
2. In small saucepan combine orange juice, honey, orange peel, and almond extract. Heat just to dissolve honey.
3. Cook and pour over fruit. Chill until serving time. Remove orange peel. Makes four servings.

Note for Brown Baggers: Place 1 cup in tight-seal container. Chill overnight.

CHOCOLATE PEANUTTY MOUSSE

1 envelope unflavored gelatin
¼ cup cold water
1 6-ounce package semisweet chocolate pieces
½ cup hot coffee
2 eggs, separated, at room temperature
¼ cup sugar
½ cup heavy cream, whipped
⅓ cup chopped, dry roasted, unsalted peanuts

1. In small custard cup, sprinkle gelatin over cold water. Let stand to soften. Place cup inside small saucepan or skillet of hot water and heat to dissolve gelatin.
2. In container of electric blender combine chocolate pieces and hot coffee. Cover and process until smooth, about 30 seconds. With blender still running slowly, pour melted gelatin through small hole in center of cover, then add egg yolks one at a time.
3. In medium size bowl with electric mixer at high speed, beat egg whites until soft peaks form. Gradually beat in sugar, a little at a time, until egg whites are stiff. In another bowl with mixer at high speed, beat heavy cream until stiff.
4. Fold chocolate mixture gently into egg whites. Then fold heavy cream and chopped peanuts into chocolate mixture. Spoon into four 6-ounce serving glasses. Makes four servings.

Note for Brown Baggers: Spoon ¾ cup Chocolate Peanutty Mousse into firm container with tight-seal lid. Chill overnight.

Nutrition Note: Chocolate is a surprising source of some iron, and peanuts do have protein, as do eggs. But in spite of these benefits, this remains a special-occasions-only addition to the lunch box, since fat and cholesterol are high.

CITRUS CINNAMON FRUIT SALAD

4 large seedless oranges
4 large red grapefruit
6 2-inch strips lemon peel
¼ cup lemon juice
¼ to ⅓ cup honey
2 3-inch cinnamon sticks

1. Using a small, sharp knife, cut peel from oranges to remove both rind and pith. Cut down between orange segments to free from membrane. Over glass measuring cup, squeeze membrane to remove any juice.
2. Similarly prepare red grapefruit segments, squeezing membrane to remove juice. Place orange and grapefruit segments in serving bowl.
3. Place lemon peel strips in small saucepan. Add lemon juice to reserved orange-grapefruit juice and enough water to measure ¾ cup. Add to saucepan along with honey to taste, and cinnamon sticks. Heat just to dissolve.
4. Pour over orange and grapefruit segments. Chill as long as possible before serving. Remove peels and cinnamon sticks. Makes four servings.

Note for Brown Baggers: Place 1 cup in tight-seal container. Chill overnight.

NO-BAKE INDIVIDUAL BLUEBERRY CHEESECAKES

- 1 envelope unflavored gelatin
- 1/4 cup cold orange juice
- 1/2 cup boiling orange juice
- 1/2 cup brown sugar, firmly packed
- 1 16-ounce container skim-milk, small-curd cottage cheese
- 2 eggs, separated
- 1 tablespoon grated orange rind
- 1 14 1/2-ounce can evaporated milk, well chilled
- 1 pint fresh blueberries or 1 16-ounce poly-bag frozen blueberries, thawed
- 3/4 cup graham cracker crumbs

1. In blender container, sprinkle gelatin over cold orange juice. Let stand to soften. Add 1/2 cup boiling orange juice and brown sugar. Process to dissolve gelatin. Add cottage cheese, egg yolks, and orange rind. Process until mixture is smooth.
2. In medium bowl with electric beater at high speed, beat evaporated milk until soft peaks form. In a small bowl beat egg whites until soft peaks form.
3. Sprinkle 2 tablespoons graham cracker crumbs in bottom of four 10-ounce dessert dishes. Add blueberries to cover crumbs (there will be some berries over). Divide cheesecake mixture evenly between dessert dishes. Sprinkle tops of each with remaining crumbs and blueberries, pressing gently so they adhere. Chill at least 2 hours or until firm and set. Makes four servings.

Note for Brown Baggers: Make one dessert directly in firm container with tight-seal lid. Chill overnight. Pack in insulated lunch box.

DRIED FRUIT COMPOTE

- 1 11-ounce package mixed dried fruit
- 1 cup dried pear halves, cut into bite-size pieces
- 1 cup dried apple rings, cut into bite-size pieces
- 1 tablespoon chopped fresh ginger (optional)
- 1 tablespoon grated orange rind
- 2 cups apple juice
- 1/2 cup orange juice
- 1 1/2 teaspoons vanilla extract

1. In large saucepan combine dried fruit, dried pear, and dried apple pieces. Stir in ginger and orange rind. Add apple juice and orange juice.
2. Bring mixture to boiling point. Reduce heat and simmer, covered, 10 minutes. Add vanilla extract and cool fruits 1 hour in saucepan. Place in large serving bowl. Cover and chill until serving time. Makes four servings.

Note for Brown Baggers: Place ¾ cup fruit mixture with juice in firm container with tight-seal lid. Chill overnight.

Nutrition Note: Make sure mixed dried fruit has some apricots for vitamin A.

FRESH LEMON WHIP

1 envelope unflavored gelatin
¼ cup cold water
4 eggs, separated
¾ cup sugar
½ cup fresh lemon juice
2 tablespoons grated lemon rind
½ cup heavy cream, stiffly beaten or ¼ cup low-fat, unflavored yogurt

1. In small custard cup sprinkle gelatin over water. Let stand to soften. In top of double boiler, over simmering (not boiling) water, combine egg yolks, ¼ cup sugar, and lemon juice. Cook, stirring constantly until sugar dissolves and mixture thickens. Stir in gelatin to dissolve, then lemon rind. Cool.
2. With electric mixer at high speed, beat egg whites until soft peaks form. Gradually beat in sugar, a little at a time, until egg whites are stiff. In another bowl with mixer at high speed, beat heavy cream until stiff.
3. Fold egg whites into cooled lemon mixture, then fold in heavy cream. Spoon mixture into serving bowl or four 1-cup serving dishes. Chill 3 hours or until firm. Makes four servings.

Note for Brown Baggers: Spoon 1 cup lemon whip into firm container with tight-seal lid. Chill overnight. Place in insulated lunch box to carry.

Nutrition Note: A traditional recipe, with sugar reduced, but still a sweet treat. For those who are nutrition conscius, substitute yogurt for heavy cream; the dessert will not be so voluminous and have more of a tangy taste. Both egg yolks and heavy cream make this a once-in-awhile dessert.

REFRESHING MELON SALAD

1 cup cantaloupe melon balls
1 cup watermelon balls
1 cup honeydew melon balls
1 or 2 kiwi fruit, peeled and thinly sliced
½ cup red grapefruit juice or orange juice
2 tablespoons honey (optional)

1. In large bowl blend together cantaloupe, watermelon, and honeydew melon balls. Peel and slice kiwi fruit. If slices are large, cut in half.
2. If melon balls are slightly underripe, beat together grapefruit or orange juice *with* honey. (If fruit is ripe, omit honey.) Pour over fruit. Cover and chill. Makes four ¾-cup servings.

Note for Brown Baggers: Place ¾ cup fruit and a little juice in salad container with tight-seal lid. Chill overnight.

Nutrition Note: A fruit dessert with high vitamin A and C content.

ORANGE SNOW

2 navel oranges
1 envelope unflavored gelatin
1½ cups orange juice
¼ to ⅓ cup sugar, depending on taste
2 egg whites

1. Using small sharp knife, cut peel from orange to remove both rind and pith. Cut down between orange segments to free from membrane. Cut each section into four pieces. Set aside.
2. In small custard cup sprinkle gelatin over ¼ cup orange juice. Let stand to soften. Place cup in small skillet or saucepan of water. Heat to dissolve gelatin.
3. Meanwhile, in medium saucepan heat orange juice and sugar, just to dissolve sugar. Stir in melted gelatin. Pour into large bowl. Cool and chill until gelatin is semiset.
4. In medium bowl with mixer at high speed, beat egg whites until very stiff. Beat semiset gelatin until foamy. Fold egg whites into gelatin mixture. Fold in reserved orange pieces, draining free of juice.
5. Divide dessert between four 10-ounce dessert dishes. Makes four servings.

Note for Brown Baggers: Make one dessert directly in firm container with tight-seal lid. Chill overnight. Pack in insulated lunch box.

Nutrition Note: A low-calorie, high vitamin C dessert.

ORIENTAL FRUIT SALAD

1 8-ounce can pineapple chunks in natural juices
1 cup honeydew melon, in ½-inch cubes
1 cup cantaloupe melon, in ½-inch cubes
¼ cup lime or lemon juice
¼ cup honey
1 teaspoon grated lime rind or anise seeds

1. Drain and reserve juice from pineapple chunks. Place pineapple, honeydew, and cantaloupe chunks in serving bowl.
2. Combine pineapple juice and lime juice, adding water to measure ¾ cup. Place in small saucepan together with honey, lime rind, or anise seeds, depending on your taste.
3. Heat just to dissolve honey. Cool and pour over fruit. Chill to serving time. Makes four servings.

Note for Brown Baggers: Place ¾ cup in tight-seal container. Chill overnight.

GINGER PEACHY SALAD

6 large peaches or nectarines
1 3½-ounce package crystallized ginger
2 2-inch strips lemon peel
2 2-inch strips orange peel
½ cup water
¼ cup lemon juice

1. Peel skin from peaches, if desired. There is no need to do this if you are using nectarines. Cut peaches or nectarines in half. Remove pit and cut halves into slices. Place in serving bowl.
2. Finely dice crystallized ginger. Place in small saucepan with lemon and orange peels, water, and lemon juice. Heat just until bubbles appear around rim. Cool, pour over peaches. Chill until serving time. Remove peels. Makes four servings.

Note for Brown Baggers: Place 1 cup in tight-seal container. Chill overnight. If crystallized ginger is not available, substitute 1 tablespoon chopped fresh ginger root or 1½ teaspoons powdered ginger. Add ¼ cup brown sugar, firmly packed, to liquids before heating to dissolve.

PINEAPPLE BERRY SALAD IN FRESH FRUIT JUICE

1 cup orange juice
1 small, ripe, fresh pineapple
½ cup fresh strawberries, sliced
½ cup cantaloupe melon cubes
½ cup fresh blueberries
½ cup green seedless grapes, halved

1. Place orange juice in blender or food processor container. Cut pineapple into fourths; cut flesh away from shells. Add flesh from one-fourth of pineapple (cut in cubes) to orange juice. Process until pureéd.
2. Pour pureéd fruit juice into serving bowl. Add remaining pineapple (cut in bite-size pieces), strawberries, melon, blueberries, and grapes. Cover and chill until serving time. Makes four servings.

Note for Brown Baggers: Place 1 cup Pineapple Berry salad in salad container with tight-seal lid. Chill overnight.

PUMPKIN CHIFFON MOUSSE

1 cup fresh or canned, unsweetened, pumpkin pureé
1 envelope unflavored gelatin
½ cup orange juice
2 tablespoons finely chopped crystallized ginger
2 teaspoons grated orange rind
3 egg whites
¼ to ⅓ cup sugar, depending on taste

1. In medium bowl beat pumpkin pureé until smooth. In custard cup sprinkle gelatin over orange juice. Let stand to soften. Place cup inside small saucepan or skillet of water and heat to dissolve.
2. Cool gelatin slightly and add to pumpkin pureé with ginger and orange rind. Chill until consistency of beaten egg whites.
3. In medium bowl with mixer at high speed, beat egg whites until soft peaks form. Slowly beat in sugar until stiff peaks form. Beat chilled pumpkin pureé until foamy.
4. Fold egg whites into pumpkin pureé. Divide dessert between four 10-ounce dessert dishes. Makes four servings.

Note for Brown Baggers: Make one dessert directly in a firm con-

STRAWBERRIES WITH STRAWBERRY CREAM

1 envelope unflavored gelatin
¼ cup cold water
1 pint fresh strawberries
1 8-ounce container low-fat, unflavored yogurt
2 tablespoons honey
1 tablespoon grated orange rind
1 teaspoon vanilla extract
½ cup heavy cream, whipped

1. In small custard cup sprinkle gelatin over cold water. Let stand to soften. Place cup inside small saucepan or skillet of water and heat to dissolve gelatin.
2. Wash, hull, and dry strawberries. In large bowl crush half strawberries to a pureé; slice remaining half and divide between four dessert dishes.
3. Stir melted gelatin into strawberry pureé. Stir in yogurt, honey, orange rind, and vanilla extract. Chill until the consistency of unbeaten egg whites. Beat with electric mixer until foamy.
4. In separate bowl beat heavy cream. Fold into strawberry-yogurt mixture. Spoon over sliced berries. Makes four servings.

Note for Brown Baggers: Make one dessert directly in a firm container with a tight-seal lid. Chill overnight. Pack in an insulated lunch box.

Nutrition Note: Strawberries are rich in vitamin C. Instead of heavy cream, fold 2 egg whites, stiffly beaten, into strawberry-yogurt mixture.

¾ cup raw, long-grain rice
2½ cups water
2 envelopes unflavored gelatin
3 cups milk or low-fat milk
⅓ to ½ cup honey or sugar
1½ teaspoons grated lemon rind
2 large, very ripe pears, preferably Bosc or Anjou pears
2 egg whites

1. In medium saucepan cook rice according to package directions, using 2 cups water. Rice should be tender and fluffy, with no liquid remaining in pan.
2. In custard cup sprinkle gelatin over remaining ½ cup water. Let stand to soften. Place cup inside small saucepan or skillet of water and heat to dissolve gelatin.
3. In large saucepan heat milk and honey just to dissolve. Stir in melted gelatin and cooked rice. Add lemon rind. Chill until mixture is semiset, about 1 hour. Stir occasionally to distribute rice evenly.
4. Meanwhile, peel pears. Cut into small dice. Fold into gelatin mixture. In small bowl with mixer at high speed, beat eggs until stiff. Fold into gelatin-pear mixture. Divide mixture between four 10-ounce dessert dishes. Makes four servings.

Note for Brown Baggers: Make one dessert directly in a firm container with a tight-seal lid. Chill overnight. Pack in an insulated lunch box.

Nutrition Note: For a high vitamin C dessert fold in 2 cups orange segments, well drained, or 2 cups sliced strawberries as an alternate to the diced pears.

QUICK SUMMER-FRUIT PIES

Filling

2 cups dark cherries, halved and pitted (about ½ pound)
2 cups fresh blueberries, washed and dried (1 pint)
⅓ cup orange juice
2 tablespoons lemon juice
½ cup brown sugar, lightly packed, or to taste
2 2-inch strips lemon peel
¾ teaspoon cinnamon
2 teaspoons cornstarch
2 tablespoons water

Topping

1 cup graham cracker crumbs
¼ cup brown sugar, lightly packed
¼ teaspoon cinnamon
¼ cup margarine, melted

1. To make filling: In a medium saucepan combine cherries and blueberries. Add orange and lemon juice, brown sugar, lemon peel, and cinnamon. Simmer, covered, 10 minutes or just until

fruit is tender. Remove lemon peel.
2. In small custard cup blend together cornstarch and water; quickly stir into fruit. Bring to boiling point, stirring constantly, until juice thickens. Divide mixture between four 10-ounce oven-proof baking dishes or dessert dishes. Let cool completely.
3. To make topping: In small bowl combine graham-craker crumbs, brown sugar, and cinnamon. Toss with melted margarine. Sprinkle ¼ cup topping over each dessert. Chill until serving time. Or bake in preheated 375°F oven for 5 minutes. Makes four servings.

Note for Brown Baggers: Place 1 cup filling in a 10-ounce individual aluminum pie pan. Top with ¼ cup graham-cracker crumb mixture. Chill overnight. Cover pie pan tightly with plastic wrap. Place inside firm container with a tight-seal lid. Pack in insulated lunch box.

Nutrition Note: Cherries and blueberries have a good supply of vitamin A. The quantity of sugar you add will depend on the sweetness of the fruit and your taste.

9
COOKIES: A SOMETIMES SWEET TREAT

From time to time an occasional sweet treat is a must in everybody's lunch box. No one refuses a good homemade cookie. If you make them at home, they are slightly less sweet than store-bought varieties, and you make sure they always have "good-for-you" ingredients—whole-grain flours and fresh and dried fruits, for example.

Here are ten homemade cookie recipes with ten variations—a wholesome addition to your family cookie jar, whether for brown bag lunches or after-school snacks.

NUTRITION KNOW-HOW:
- Always use a polyunsaturated cholesterol- and salt-free margarine when making cookies. Read the box label carefully to find out.
- Sugar is sugar, no matter whether brown, granulated, or honey. Train your family to enjoy cookies that are less sweet.
- Use dried and fresh fruits to add natural sweetness to cookies. More importantly, fruits have fiber, vitamins, and minerals.
- Use whole grains, particularly oatmeal, wherever possible. Again, the benefit is fiber.
- No one pretends cookies are a big nutritional plus to the lunch box. But these homemade ones do have less refined flour, sugar, and fat than store-bought ones. Nonetheless, serve sparingly.

Consumer Notes on Cookies

Successful baking always requires care and attention. For perfect cookies, go through the following check list.
- Check oven temperature for accuracy. Hang an independent oven thermometer on the middle rack of the oven to verify the thermostat reading. Ovens vary as much as 50°F either way.
- Check to see that you have the correct size baking pans. If using oven-proof glass baking dishes, reduce temperature by 25°F. These dishes bake faster.

- Measure ingredients accurately. Use metal cups for dry ingredients and glass measures for liquid ingredients.
- Follow baking and cooling instructions completely and, once cookies are cooled, store in an air-tight container.
- No-bake cookies should be stored in the refrigerator until packing.

Pack cookies safely by wrapping in foil or plastic wrap to keep crisp. Also, put in a rigid container to prevent them from being crushed. No-bake cookies must be kept cool in an insulated lunch box.

PEANUT BALLS

1 cup margarine
1/3 cup confectioners' sugar
1 teaspoon vanilla extract
1 cup sifted all-purpose flour

1 cup finely chopped unsalted, dry-roasted peanuts
1/2 cup ground unsalted, dry-roasted peanuts

1. In medium bowl with mixer at high speed, beat together margarine, sugar, and vanilla extract.
2. Stir in flour and finely chopped peanuts to make a soft dough. Roll dough into cookies, using 2 teaspoons dough for each. Lightly floured hands will help this process.
3. Place peanut balls on lightly greased cookie sheets. Chill at least 30 minutes.
4. Preheat oven to 350°F. Bake cookies 20 minutes. Place on wire rack to cool. While warm, lightly sprinkle with ground peanuts (i.e., 1 cup peanuts processed in blender or food processor to 1/2 cup fine powder). Cool completely. Makes approximately 60 cookies.

Variation: Walnut Balls: 1 cup finely chopped walnuts and 1/2 cup *ground* walnuts may be substituted for the peanuts in the above recipe.

BANANA BROWNIES

1 cup all-purpose flour
1 cup light brown sugar, firmly packed
1/3 cup margarine
1 1/2 teaspoons baking powder
1 egg, lightly beaten

1 cup coarsely mashed banana
1 6-ounce package semisweet chocolate pieces
2 teaspoons grated lemon rind

1. Preheat oven to 350°F. Grease a 9-inch square baking pan.
2. In large bowl with mixer at low speed, blend flour, sugar, and margarine until mixture resembles coarse cornmeal. Blend in baking powder. Stir in egg and banana.
3. Gently fold in chocolate pieces and lemon rind (add a little milk if batter is stiff). Spread mixture in baking pan. Bake 25 to 30 minutes or until cake tester or toothpick inserted in center comes out clean. Cool in pan on wire rack. Cut into 1½-inch squares. Makes 36 brownies.

Variation: Pumpkin Brownies: 1 cup unsweetened pumpkin pureé from 1 16-ounce can may be substituted for the banana in the above recipe.

CHOCOLATE FRUIT BARS

1 6-ounce package semisweet chocolate chips
½ cup margarine
½ cup dark brown sugar, firmly packed

1½ cups all-purpose flour
1 teaspoon baking powder

Topping

1 cup chopped toasted almonds
½ cup finely diced dried apricots

½ cup chopped dark raisins
2 eggs, slightly beaten
1 tablespoon grated orange rind

1. Preheat oven to 350°F. Grease a 13 × 9 × 2-inch baking pan. In top of double boiler over hot (not boiling) water, melt chocolate chips, margarine, and sugar. Stir well to mix.
2. Combine flour and baking powder. Stir into chocolate mixture. Spread batter evenly in prepared pan. Bake 20 minutes and remove from oven.
3. Meanwhile, make topping by combinine almonds, apricots, raisins, eggs, and orange rind. Spread evenly over hot cookie dough. Return to oven; bake 20 minutes more. Cool in pan on wire rack. Cut into 2-inch squares. Makes 24 cookies.

BUTTERSCOTCH APPLE BARS

1 6-ounce package butterscotch chips
½ cup margarine
½ cup dark brown sugar, firmly packed

1½ cups all-purpose flour
1 teaspoon baking powder

Topping

1 cup chopped walnuts or pecans
½ cup diced dried apples
½ cup chopped golden raisins

2 eggs, slightly beaten
1 tablespoon grated orange rind

1. Preheat oven to 350°F. Grease a 13 × 9 × 2-inch baking pan. Proceed as in previous recipe, melting butterscotch chips, margarine, and sugar, then adding flour and baking powder to make a batter. Bake as directed.
2. Make topping as directed in previous recipe using walnuts, apples, raisins, eggs, and orange rind. Spread topping on cookie base. Bake as directed. Makes 24 cookies.

OATMEAL CARROT COOKIES

½ cup margarine
½ cup honey
1 egg
1 cup uncooked, quick-cooking oats
1 cup all-purpose flour

1 teaspoon baking powder
½ teaspoon baking soda
1 cup grated carrot
¾ cup chopped pecans
2 teaspoons grated orange rind

1. Preheat oven to 350°F. Lightly grease large cookie sheet. In large bowl with mixer at high speed, beat margarine, honey, and egg until well-blended. Stir in oats.
2. Sift together flour, baking powder, and baking soda. Fold into honey mixture together with carrot, pecans, and orange rind.
3. Drop mixture by heaping teaspoonsful onto cookie sheets, spacing 2 inches apart. Bake 10 to 12 minutes or until lightly brown. Remove to wire rack to cool immediately.

Variation: Oatmeal Zucchini Cookies: Using grated raw zucchini pressed free of liquid and measured to 1 cup, instead of grated carrots, proceed as in previous recipe. Makes 48 cookies.

OLD-FASHIONED OATMEAL COOKIES

1 cup margarine
1 cup sugar
2 cups uncooked, old-fashioned oats
2 cups all-purpose flour
2 teaspoons cinnamon
1 teaspoon baking soda
½ teaspoon baking powder
¾ cup low-fat, unflavored yogurt
1 cup chopped walnuts
1 cup chopped dark raisins

1. Preheat oven to 350°F. Heavily grease large cookie sheet.
2. In large bowl with mixer at high speed, beat margarine until soft. Beat in sugar. Stir in oatmeal and the flour that has been sifted with cinnamon, baking soda, and baking powder.
3. Gently fold in ¼ cup yogurt. Add half of walnuts and raisins. Add remaining yogurt, walnuts, and raisins alternately. Yogurt should be added just to achieve a soft dough.
4. Drop by heaping tablespoonsful onto cookie sheet, spacing 2 inches apart. Bake about 12 at a time. Bake 20 minutes until deep golden brown. Let cool on cookie sheet 3 minutes. Remove to wire rack to cool, using a spatula. Makes 36 cookies.

Variation: Applesauce-Oatmeal Cookies: Substitute ¾ cup unsweetened applesauce for yogurt in above recipe. Make and bake cookies as in previous recipe. Makes 36 cookies.

PEANUT DATE CHEWS

2 cups all-purpose flour
1 cup granulated sugar
1 cup margarine
1 cup unsalted, dry roasted peanuts
1 16-ounce package pitted dates, finely chopped
3 to 4 tablespoons honey or maple syrup
1 tablespoon grated orange rind

1. Preheat oven to 400°F. Lightly grease 9-inch square baking pan.
2. In large bowl with mixer at low speed, blend flour, sugar, and margarine. Mixture should resemble coarse cornmeal. Set aside.
3. In blender or food processor process nuts until a fine powder. (If using blender process only ½ cup at a time.) Add half of nuts to flour mixture.
4. Blend remaining nuts with chopped dates. Add enough honey to make a soft preserve-like consistency. Stir in orange rind.
5. Firmly pat half of flour-nut mixture in bottom of pan. Spread date

mixture over base. Top with remaining flour-nut mixture, sprinkling lightly. Bake 25 to 30 minutes. Cool in pan on wire rack. Cut into 1½-inch squares. Makes 36 cookies.

Variation: Peanutty Mixed Fruit Chews: Using 2 cups finely diced, mixed dried fruit (a combination of apricots, figs, and dark raisins is good) instead of pitted chopped dates, proceed as in previous recipe. Makes 36 cookies.

APPLE DROP COOKIES

½ cup margarine
1 cup brown sugar, firmly packed
1 egg
½ cup unsweetened apple sauce
1 teaspoon vanilla extract

2½ cups all-purpose flour
1½ teaspoons cinnamon
½ teaspoon baking soda
1 cup grated fresh apple, pressed free of juice
1 cup chopped walnuts

1. Preheat oven to 375°F. Have ready a large, *ungreased* cookie sheet.
2. In large bowl with mixer at high speed, beat margarine and sugar until soft. Beat in egg, applesauce, and vanilla extract.
3. Sift together flour, cinnamon, and baking soda. Gently stir into applesauce mixture. Then stir in grated apple and walnuts.
4. Drop by tablespoonsful onto cookie sheet, spacing 2 inches apart. Bake 10 minutes or until light golden brown. Remove from cookie sheet to wire rack to cool immediately. Makes approximately 48 cookies.

Variation: Ginger-Pear Drop Cookies: Using 1½ teaspoons powdered ginger instead of cinnamon and 1 cup grated fresh pear instead of fresh apple, proceed as directed in previous recipe.

NO-BAKE CHOCOLATE MELTAWAYS

1 cup margarine
1 1-ounce square unsweetened chocolate, cut up
¼ cup brown sugar, firmly packed
1 egg, beaten

½ teaspoon vanilla extract
2 cups graham cracker crumbs
¾ cup finely diced dried apricots
¾ cup slivered almonds

Frosting

4 1-ounce squares unsweetened chocolate, cut up

1. In top of double boiler over simmering water, melt margarine. Add cut-up chocolate; stir to melt.
2. Remove from heat; cool slightly. Stir in brown sugar, egg, and vanilla extract. Blend in graham cracker crumbs, apricots, and almonds.
3. Press into 13 × 9 × 2-inch baking pan. Chill 2 hours. In top of double boiler over simmering water, make frosting by melting chocolate. Spread over top of chilled cookie mixture. Cut into 2-inch squares while frosting is soft. Chill 1 hour more. Cover with foil. Keep chilled in refrigerator until needed. Makes 24 cookies.

Variation: No-Bake Crispy Meltaways:

1 cup margarine
1 1-ounce square unsweetened chocolate, cut up
¼ cup brown sugar, firmly packed
1 egg, beaten
½ teaspoon almond extract
2 cups unsweetened, crisp, ready-to-eat cereal, coarsely crushed
1½ cups golden raisins, chopped

Frosting

4 1-ounce squares unsweetened chocolate, cut up

1. Make cookies as in previous recipe, substituting crushed ready-to-eat cereal for graham-cracker crumbs and golden raisins for apricots and almonds.
2. Chill and frost cookies as in previous recipe. Makes 24 cookies.

NOTE: Crushed, crisp rice cereal or cornflakes, or any multi-grained, crisp cereal, is excellent in this recipe.

WHOLE-WHEAT SHORT BREAD

1 cup margarine, softened
½ cup granulated sugar
1 cup *unsifted* all-purpose flour
1 cup *unsifted* whole-wheat flour

1. In large bowl, beat margarine until soft. Beat in sugar.
2. With wooden spoon, stir in flour. Mixture will be very stiff, and you may knead the last of the flour in with your hands. The dough should form a ball and leave the sides of the bowl clean.
3. Divide dough into three parts. Roll out each on an ungreased cookie sheet to form a 5-inch circle. Pinch edges to flute and mark each circle lightly into 8 pie-shaped wedges. Chill short bread 30 minutes.
4. Preheat oven to 325°F. Bake short bread 25 minutes or until golden brown. Cool on cookie sheets on wire racks, cutting short bread all the way through into wedges while hot. Store in an airtight container. Makes 24 cookies.

Variation: Oatmeal Short Bread:

1 cup margarine, softened
½ cup granulated sugar

1 cup all-purpose flour
1 to 1¼ cup uncooked, quick-cooking oats

1. Make short bread as in previous recipe, kneading in oatmeal to achieve a dry dough. Since oatmeal is light with large flakes, knead firmly and be prepared to add a little more if required.
2. Chill and bake short bread as directed in previous recipe. Makes 24 cookies.

10
"GO-POWER" SUPER SNACKS

When you need to pick a snack that has a good nutritional boost, these are recipes to consider. For a midmorning pickup or an after-school pre-sports energizer, choose one of the following for an added "go-power" treat.

Some snacks are concentrated nutrition in a vacuum flask, some are nutritious nibbles to fill the empty space before or after lunch. And a few are no-bake or quick-bake substantial fare to be eaten when the workday goes on longer than usual.

NUTRITION KNOW-HOW:
- Drinks that have real substance are pureé of fruits with high vitamin A and C content.
- Rely on the natural sweetness of the fruit for palate appeal, adding sugar only as needed and in as little quantity as possible.
- Keep fat content of drinks low by using low-fat milk or milk products. These products are rich in vitamins A and D and calcium.
- Fiber is the bonus of using fresh fruits and vegetables.
- Vegetables can be made into a nutritional, boosting pureé, too. Select vegetables with high vitamin A and C content—carrots, spinach, tomatoes. They are good changes of pace for people who do not like sweet drinks.
- Out-of-hand snacks have good fiber content from most of the ingredients from which they are made.
- Nuts have vitamin B and dried apricots vitamin A. All dried fruits have natural sugar for a quick boost of energy.
- All snacks are designed to give a concentrated energy supply in a single serving with the bonus of added vitamins and mineral content.
- These snacks, however, are not designed to be "complete" meal substitutes.

Consumer Notes on Go-Power Snacks
- Pack all cold liquids in prechilled vacuum containers, if you make them instantly.
- If you can, make cold drinks ahead and chill before packing.

- Out-of-hand, crisp snacks should be packed in air-tight containers.
- No-bake snacks need to be kept chilled in order to retain their texture. Wrap individually before packing.
- Baked snacks should be wrapped individually and packed in a non-crushable container.

GRANOLA BARS

4 cups quick-cooking oats
1 cup unsalted, dry-roasted peanuts, coarsely chopped
1 cup snipped dates
1 cup dehydrated banana slices, coarsely crushed
1 teaspoon cinnamon
½ cup honey
½ cup margarine
2 egg whites

1. Preheat oven to 350°F. Heavily grease a 9 × 9-inch baking pan.
2. In large bowl toss together quick-cooking oats, chopped peanuts, snipped dates, and crushed banana slices. Sprinkle with powdered cinnamon; toss again. In small saucepan heat honey and margarine just to melt. Stir to blend well. Drizzle evenly over dry ingredients, tossing to mix well.
3. In medium bowl with electric mixer at high speed, beat egg whites until stiff. Fold into oat mixture. Press granola into prepared pan. Bake 25 to 30 minutes or until golden brown.
4. Remove pan from oven. Press mixture with broad metal spatula. Cool slightly; cut into 3 × 1½-inch bars. Let cool in pan completely.
5. Wrap each bar individually in plastic wrap to keep air-tight. Store at room temperature in air-tight container or freeze. Makes 18 3 × 1½-inch bars.

WHOLE-WHEAT NUT BARS

1 cup crisp whole-wheat cereal, crushed
½ cup all-purpose flour
½ cup whole-wheat flour
½ cup brown sugar, firmly packed
2 teaspoons baking powder
1 egg
¼ cup vegetable oil
¾ cup milk or low-fat milk
½ cup chopped peanuts
½ cup chopped walnuts
½ cup sunflower seeds

1. Preheat oven to 350°F. Grease a 9 × 9-inch baking pan liberally.
2. In large bowl blend crushed cereal, all-purpose flour, whole-wheat flour, brown sugar, and baking powder. Make a well in center of dry ingredients.
3. Beat together egg and oil. Add to dry ingredients together with milk. Stir until just moistened. Fold in peanuts, walnuts, and sunflower seeds.
4. Spoon batter into prepared pan. Bake 35 to 40 minutes or until cake tester inserted in center comes out clean. Cool completely in pan on wire rack. Makes 18 1½-inch squares.

CARROT WHEAT BISCUITS

1 cup all-purpose flour
1 cup crisp whole-wheat cereal, crushed (about 1½ cups bite-size pieces)
4 teaspoons baking powder
½ cup finely grated carrot
3 tablespoons vegetable oil
½ cup milk or low-fat milk
1 tablespoon sesame seed

1. Preheat oven to 400°F.
2. In large bowl combine flour, crushed cereal, and baking powder. Stir in grated carrot. Make a well in center of dry ingredients.
3. Beat together oil and milk. Add to center of dry ingredients; stir in just until moistened.
4. Turn onto lightly floured surface, knead 10 times. Pat into ¾-inch thick circle. Using 2½-inch cutter, cut out 12 biscuits. Dough will have to be rerolled for a second cutting.
5. Place biscuits on ungreased cookie sheet. Sprinkle with sesame seeds. Makes 12 2½-inch biscuits.

"YOGURT" BANANA BITES

2 cups non-fat, dry powdered milk
½ cup dehydrated banana slices, finely crushed
½ cup powdered sugar
2 teaspoons grated lemon rind
⅓ cup margarine, melted
1 to 2 tablespoons lemon juice

Coating (optional)

1 8-ounce bar "carob chocolate"
2 tablespoons margarine

1. In large bowl blend powdered milk, crushed bananas, sugar, and lemon rind.
2. Melt margarine; cool slightly and, using a fork, toss into dry ingredients. Using finger tips, press mixture together to form a soft but pliable dough, adding lemon juice to achieve correct consistency.
3. On a surface sprinkled lightly with powdered milk, shape into bars 1 × 1 × 1¼ inches. Wrap in individual squares of plastic wrap. Chill until needed.
4. If desired melt "carob chocolate" and margarine in top of double boiler, over simmering water. Placing Yogurt Banana Bites on a fork, one at a time, dip into coating to cover completely.
5. Set on wire cake rack. Chill to form coating. Wrap and store as above until needed. Makes approximately 12 "bites".

PEANUT BUTTERS

2 cups graham cracker crumbs
¼ to ⅓ cup brown sugar, firmly packed
⅔ cup creamy peanut butter
½ cup unsalted, dry-roasted peanuts, finely chopped
1½ teaspoons grated orange rind

1. In large bowl combine graham cracker crumbs and brown sugar, according to taste. Using two knives or pastry cutter, cut in peanut butter until mixture resembles coarse crumbs.
2. Stir in finely chopped peanuts and orange rind. Press 2 tablespoons mixture into 12-hole (1½-inch) paper-lined gem pan. Chill at least 2 hours. Wrap individually in plastic wrap before adding to an insulated lunch box. Makes 12 Peanut Butters.

NO-BAKE SUPER BROWNIES

2 cups graham cracker crumbs
½ cup walnuts, pecans or almonds, chopped
½ cup chocolate chips, coarsely chopped
½ cup brown sugar, firmly packed
½ cup margarine
1 1-ounce square semisweet chocolate

1. In large bowl combine graham cracker crumbs, nuts, chocolate chips, and sugar.
2. In small bowl over hot water, melt margarine and chocolate, stir-

ring to combine. Do not heat longer than necessary to melt. (This can be done in a double boiler.)
3. Drizzle melted chocolate mixture over dry ingredients. Toss with a fork to blend well. Press mixture into a lightly greased 9 × 9-inch baking pan, or press ¼ cup mixture into 12-hole (2½-inch) muffin pan lined with paper baking liners.
4. Chill at least 2 hours. Cut brownies in pan into 18 1½-inch squares. Wrap all brownies in plastic wrap before adding to an insulated lunch box. Makes 12 or 18 brownies.

PEANUT BUTTER MUFFINS WITH CHEESE FILLING

1 cup all-purpose flour
1 cup yellow cornmeal
4 teaspoons baking powder

½ cup creamly peanut butter
¾ cup milk or low-fat milk
1 egg
⅓ cup low-fat cottage cheese

1. Preheat oven to 400°F. Heavily grease one 12-hole (2½-inch) muffin pan, and line with paper baking liners.
2. In large bowl combine flour, cornmeal, and baking powder. Using two knives or a pastry blender, cut in peanut butter to cornmeal mixture. Mixture should resemble coarse crumbs.
3. In 1 cup measure beat together milk and egg. Add all at once to dry ingredients. Stir just until moistened. Fill each muffin hole ⅓ full with batter.
4. Place 1 teaspoon cottage cheese in center of each hole, top with more batter to fill ⅔ full.
5. Bake 20 minutes or until golden. Remove immediately from pan to wire rack to cool. Makes 12 2½-inch muffins.

NUTRITIOUS SAVORY NIBBLES

2 cups bite-size whole-wheat cereal
1 12-ounce can Spanish peanuts
½ cup sunflower or pumpkin seeds

⅓ cup margarine
2 teaspoons dried dill weed or basil
¼ teaspoon curry powder or chili powder (optional)

1. Preheat oven to 325°F. In medium bowl blend cereal, peanuts, and sunflower or pumpkin seeds.

2. In small saucepan melt margarine. Add dried dill or basil and curry powder or chili powder, if desired. Drizzle over dry ingredients.
3. Press mixture evenly in ungreased 15 × 9 × 1-inch jelly-roll pan. Bake 30 to 40 minutes to crisp, heat, and flavor mixture, stirring ingredients every 10 minutes.
4. Let cool in pan completely before storing in air-tight container to use as needed. Makes 3 cups mixture.

BLAZE-THE-TRAIL SNACK

1 cup unsalted, dry-roasted peanuts
1 cup dark raisins
1 cup soft-pack, dried apricot halves, cut in slivers
1 cup dehydrated banana slices
3 orange peel strips, ½-inch wide × 3 inches long

1. In large plastic bag combine peanuts, raisins, apricots, and banana slices. Shake to mix well.
2. Place in air-tight container together with orange strips. Store 2 to 3 days before using so dried fruits will become moist and have an orange flavor. Pack ½ cup in air-tight plastic bag as an out-of-hand snack. Makes eight ½-cup servings.

Nutrition Note: Do not be tempted to put coconut in this snack. Coconut contains saturated fat, a nutritional negative.

PUMPKIN APRICOT SQUARES

¼ cup brown sugar, firmly packed
⅓ cup margarine
2 eggs
1 cup canned pumpkin
⅓ cup milk or low-fat milk
1½ cups all-purpose flour
½ cup whole-wheat flour
2 teaspoons baking powder
1 teaspoon cinnamon
½ teaspoon baking soda
¾ cup snipped dried apricots
¾ cup chopped walnuts

1. Preheat oven to 350°F. Well-grease and flour 9 × 9-inch baking pan.
2. In large bowl with electric mixer at high speed, beat sugar and margarine until light and fluffy. Beat in eggs. At low speed beat in pumpkin and milk.

3. In medium bowl blend all-purpose flour, whole-wheat flour, baking powder, cinnamon, and baking soda. Stir into pumpkin mixture.
4. Fold in apricots and walnuts. Spoon batter into prepared pan. Bake 35 to 40 minutes or until cake tester inserted in center comes out clean. Cool completely in pan on wire rack. Makes 18 1½-inch squares.

Nutrition Note: A less-sweet-than-normal snack with a good vitamin A boost.

HOT ORANGE BOOSTER

1 tablespoon instant, iron-fortified, ready-to-cook cereal
1 cup milk or low-fat milk
1 egg
3 tablespoons orange juice concentrate
1 tablespoon honey (optional)

1. In small saucepan blend cereal and milk. Bring to boiling point, stirring constantly.
2. Pour into blender container. Cover. With blender running, add egg and orange juice concentrate through small hole in top of blender cover.
3. Add honey, if desired. Makes one 1½-cup serving.

STRAWBERRY CREAM

1 8-ounce container low-fat, unflavored yogurt
1 egg
1 cup fresh strawberries, sliced
½ cup non-fat dried milk powder
1 tablespoon honey (optional)
½ teaspoon vanilla extract

1. In container of electric blender combine unflavored yogurt, egg, and strawberries. Cover and blend at high speed until smooth.
2. Add milk powder, honey if desired, and vanilla extract. Cover and blend 30 seconds longer. Makes one 1¾-cup serving.

Note: 1 cup frozen strawberries, thawed (from a 16-ounce poly-bag frozen unsweetened strawberries), may be used instead of fresh berries.

THE VITAMIN A TEAM DRINK

1 8-ounce can apricot halves packed in water, drained
1 8-ounce can sliced peaches packed in natural syrup
½ cup ripe cantaloupe, coarsely chopped
1 tablespoon lemon juice
1 teaspoon grated lemon rind

1. In blender of electric container combine drained apricots and undrained peaches. Cover and blend until smooth.
2. Add cantaloupe, lemon juice, and lemon rind. Cover and blend until smooth. Makes one 1¾-cup serving.

VITAMIN C HIGH

1 cup orange juice
1 small grapefruit, peeled and segmented
½ cup fresh strawberries, sliced
½ cup cantaloupe melon, coarsely chopped

1. In container of electric blender combine orange juice and grapefruit segments. Cover and blend at high speed until smooth.
2. Add sliced strawberries and chopped cantaloupe melon. Cover and blend 30 seconds longer. Makes one 2-cup serving.

Note: For convenience or as a substitute for out-of-season fruit, use ½ cup grapefruit juice and ½ cup frozen strawberries thawed.

Nutrition Note: Very ripe, sliced papaya—when in season and not too exotic for your taste and pocketbook—would give this drink another vitamin C boost. Substitute ½ cup sliced papaya for the grapefruit, or add along with all other ingredients.

TIGER'S MILK

1½ cups milk or low-fat milk
1 envelope dry active yeast
¼ cup wheat germ
¼ cup creamy peanut butter
2 tablespoons honey (optional)

1. In small saucepan heat milk until just warm. Place yeast in container of electric blender. Pour in milk; cover, and blend to dissolve yeast.

2. Add wheat germ, peanut butter, and honey, if desired. Cover and blend until smooth. Makes one 1¾-cup serving.

ORANGE NOG

1 cup orange juice
1 egg

½ cup non-fat dry milk powder
½ cup vanilla-flavored ice milk or ice cream

1. In the container of an electric blender, combine orange juice, egg, and dry milk powder. Cover and blend at high speed until smooth.
2. Add ice milk; cover, and blend 30 seconds longer. Makes one 1¾-cup serving.

APRICOT WHEAT-GERM PURÉE

1 8-ounce can apricot halves, packed in water, drained
1 cup milk, low-fat milk, or buttermilk
¼ cup wheat germ

1 tablespoon honey (optional)
¼ teaspoon powdered cinnamon

1. In container of electric blender combine drained apricots and milk. Cover and blend at high speed until smooth.
2. Add wheat germ, honey if desired, and powdered cinnamon. Cover and blend until smooth. Makes one 1½-cup serving.

Note: In season use ¾ cup sliced and pitted fresh apricots instead of canned apricots.

BANANA PEANUT SHAKE

1 cup milk or low-fat milk
1 small ripe banana, peeled and sliced

2 tablespoons creamy peanut butter
1 tablespoon honey (optional)

1. In container of an electric blender combine ½ cup milk, sliced banana, and peanut butter. Cover and blend at high speed until smooth.

2. Add remaining milk through small hole in top of blender. Cover while blender is running. Add honey, if desired. Makes one 2-cup serving.

Note: For a hot banana drink, bring 1 cup milk to boiling point, and then do as directed above.

SPINACH POWER

1 pound fresh spinach leaves
1½ cup buttermilk or milk
1 to 2 tablespoons lemon juice
1½ teaspoon grated lemon rind
1 teaspoon nutmeg
¼ teaspoon pepper

1. Wash spinach in cold water, changing water at least twice to remove any sand. Drain. Discard coarse stems and discolored leaves. Place in covered saucepan, adding no water. Cook over low heat 3 to 5 minutes or until tender.
2. Drain spinach, pressing lightly to remove a little excess liquid. Cool and chop. Place in container of electric blender and add buttermilk. Cover and blend until smooth.
3. Add lemon juice, lemon rind, nutmeg, and pepper. Cover and blend 30 seconds longer. Chill before serving. Makes two 1½-cup servings.

Note: This drink takes more time than the others and must be prepared ahead. It is not worth doing for a single serving, so the dish makes enough for two.

Nutrition Note: Spinach is a good source of vitamin A; the milk content provides calcium and vitamins A, B, and D. Not for everyone, but a cool thirst quencher on a hot day. It can also be a cold soup.

11
QUICK NUTRITION "FIX-ITS" FOR THE BROWN BAG LUNCH

Zesty spreads and good-for-you tasty snacks are easy to pop into your lunch box. Have a supply on hand in your refrigerator, and use to boost a brown bag lunch that somehow seems in the nutritional doldrums.

All are based on very familiar lunch box products—margarine, cheese, peanut butter, and yogurt. A new flavor twist, a surprise ingredient combination, is all that is needed to encourage better eating habits. Here are over thirty, fast, nutritional flavor "fix-its" for your brown bag luncher—from the peanut-butter-and-jelly addict to the dieter who knows the virtues of skim-milk cottage cheese but wishes for a new taste—with enough to appeal to every age and every mealstyle.

NUTRITION KNOW-HOW:
These are very specific and explained at the beginning of every spread or snack recipe.

Consumer Tips for Nutrition "Fix-Its"
All are stored in the refrigerator and designed to be "on hand" as needed; most are "make ahead" except where specified. *To pack safely* make sure all go into an insulated lunch box, and, where specified, a wide-mouth, insulated container. No one wants peanut-butter-and-jelly soup.

BETTER BREAD SPREADS:
Unfortunately for the nutritionally-aware brown bag luncher, the good taste of butter is a sometime treat, if not an ingredient to be avoided altogether. Saturated fat and cholesterol are products federal dietary guidelines urge us to program out of our diet. Beyond that, we are advised to reduce the fat content of our meals.

So remember, good nutrition in the area of dairy products is a bit of a juggling game. While high in fat, dairy products are an excellent and essential source of vitamins A and D, calcium, and protein. Our opinion: use margarine (a polyunsaturated one) and low-fat dairy products that have been vitamin A and D fortified.

So for the better bread spread, take ½ cup softened, sweet, no-salt, no-cholesterol margarine and blend in 1 tablespoon lemon juice and ½ teaspoon grated lemon rind; then add:
- 1 to 2 tablespoons prepared spicy or mild mustard, depending on taste;
- 2 tablespoons fresh chopped herbs, preferably parsley, dill, or chives;
- 2 tablespoons finely chopped sour pickles, very well drained;
- 2 teaspoons dried crumbled oregano, basil, or thyme leaves;
- 1 teaspoon dry mustard, curry powder, or paprika; or
- 4 to 8 drops hot pepper sauce, depending on taste.

These flavor elements can also be added to ½ cup sour cream (which has fewer calories than margarine) or ½ cup calorie-reduced mayonnaise. "Fat-reduced" means lower in calories, but—part of the nutritional juggling game again—since these products are animal-fat based, they have some saturated fat and cholesterol.

CRACKERS AND CHEESE:

Crisp baked breads and cheese are possibly the world's first portable meal—easy to carry and certainly nonperishable. Crisp breads and crackers are always a good staple for the lunch box, as is cheese with all its many flavors and textures.

The nutrition-wise know that whole-grain crackers are best. Look for those with low-salt content, too. As for cheese, feature the skim-milk or low-fat varieties more frequently, if not always, in your midday meal. It cannot be emphasized sufficiently that cheese supplies vitamins A and D, calcium, and protein—particularly important food nutrients for growing children, teenagers, and older people.

Skim-milk or low-fat cottage cheese is a well-established lunch box item, especially for dieters. Whether used as a salad or a sandwich spread, cottage cheese combines with so many different ingredients and flavors it can be eaten at midday with more frequency than other foods. And, if cleverly fixed, there is a good chance it won't become boring.

So take 1 8-ounce container skim-milk or low-fat cottage cheese and add one of the following ingredient choices.

FOR SALADS:
- 1 tablespoon prepared spicy mustard and ½ cup finely diced cooked turkey or chicken;
- 1 tablespoon chopped fresh mint (or 1½ teaspoons dried) and

- ½ cup melon cubes or balls, preferably cantaloupe;
- 1 teaspoon curry powder, ½ cup diced, cooked, leftover meat (ham is traditional, but chicken and turkey make better nutritional sense), 1 8-ounce can crushed pineapple in natural juices, well-drained;
- 2 tablespoons chopped fresh dill weed (or 1½ teaspoons dried) and 1 3½-ounce can salmon, well drained and flaked;
- 1 small celery stalk and leaves, finely chopped, and 1 hard-cooked egg, coarsely chopped; or
- ¾ cup chopped fresh vegetables—carrots, celery, green and red peppers, or a mixture of these.

Note: Do not season any of these salads with salt; instead use grated lemon rind, lemon juice, black pepper, or hot pepper sauce to taste.

FOR SANDWICH SPREADS:
- ¼ cup chopped celery leaves and ½ teaspoon celery seeds;
- ¼ cup finely chopped olives—green, pimiento-stuffed, or black, well-drained;
- ¼ cup grated Parmesan cheese and 1 teaspoon Italian herb seasoning;
- ¼ cup apple or prune butter and 1 teaspoon powdered cinnamon;
- 2 tablespoons prepared horseradish, well drained; or
- 2 tablespoons each toasted sesame seeds and/or poppy seeds.

Note: Add crisp lettuce and tomato slices, or apple and pear slices (brushed with lemon juice to prevent discoloring) to give texture and crunch to the sandwiches.

PEANUT BUTTER AND . . .

Saltine crackers (the saltless top variety, of course), a scoop of peanut butter, plus a dab of grape jelly are a firm lunch box favorite. Better yet, peanut butter on a whole-grain cracker pleases the nutrition-conscious luncher even more.

Peanut butter can be blended with a variety of nutritious ingredients and stored in a jar in the refrigerator to swirl, as needed, on bread, crackers, or even to fill firm vegetables, such as celery, or firm, hollowed-out fruit, such as apples, or to spread between apple slices.

So take 1 cup crunchy or creamy peanut peanut butter and add:
- 1 small, ripe banana mashed with 1 tablespoon lemon juice and 1 teaspoon grated lemon rind;
- ½ cup sugar-reduced jam or jelly—preferably orange, apricot, or strawberry, though grape jelly is traditional;

- ½ cup finely chopped, dry-roasted, unsalted peanuts, almonds, or walnuts;
- ½ cup finely diced dried fruit—preferably diced apricots, dark raisins, or dates;
- ½ cup well drained, finely chopped chutney; or
- ¼ cup finely grated carrot, ¼ cup finely chopped fresh pineapple (or crushed pineapple, packed in natural juices, drained).

Note: ½ cup *very* crisp, fried, crumbled bacon and 1 to 2 tablespoons finely chopped onion make a great peanut butter blend. But bacon will make this an infrequent treat.

YOGURT AND . . .

Yogurt, an old-world ingredient that has acquired new popularity, is found in most people's brown bag lunch with remarkable frequency. Even the tough guys, whether six or sixty, know it is refreshing and, more importantly, good for you. As with any milk-based product, the nutrient values are vitamins A and D, calcium, and protein.

For maximum nutritional benefit choose low-fat, unflavored yogurt and add fresh fruits and vegetables to make a really good snack. Many commercial fruit-flavored yogurts, as well as fruit, contain quantities of refined sugar and starch—all adding unnecessary calories as well as refined (as opposed to the better, complex) carbohydrates.

Take 1 8-ounce container low-fat, unflavored yogurt and add:
- ¼ to ½ cup finely chopped cantaloupe melon, well drained;
- ¼ cup finely chopped apricots or nectarines;
- ¼ cup finely chopped strawberries;
- ¼ cup finely chopped dried apricots or dark raisins; or
- ¼ cup pumpkin pureé and 1 teaspoon lemon juice.

Note: If you *must* add sugar (even though fruit, particularly dried fruit, contains good amounts of natural sugar), blend in honey, 1 teaspoon at a time. Train your palate to enjoy the natural flavor of fruit with less, if any, added sugar. "Sweet" spices, such as cinnamon, ginger, nutmeg, and allspice—even a touch of powdered coffee—lessen the need for sugar. So does a gratering of orange rind.

YOGURT SALAD SNACKS:

Take 1 8-ounce container low-fat, unflavored yogurt and add: ¼ to ½ cup chopped fresh vegetables—tomatoes, cucumbers (both well drained), grated carrots, chopped celery, zucchini, summer squash, and red or green peppers are best. A mixture of these vegetables may be added.

Note: Season these salad snacks with grated lemon rind, lemon juice, and black pepper. Fresh herbs, such as mint, parsley, basil, or dill are excellent. Use 2 tablespoons fresh herbs or 1 tablespoon dried.

To pack yogurt snacks: Yogurt snacks must be eaten cold. Fruit and vegetables that are not too juicy may be added to yogurt and chilled overnight. Juicy strawberries or tomatoes and cucumbers should be blended at the last moment. *All* must be packed in a 12- to 16-ounce wide-mouthed vacuum container, so they may be kept very cold and eaten easily. *Do not* try to return to the original container. It is too small *and* is not insulated.

12
LUNCH BOX MENUS

All these menus have been designed from recipes within the preceding chapters. Consult the book index to locate the precise recipe mentioned.

BROWN BAG LUNCHES WITH KID-APPEAL

Menu 1:

>Beef Vegetable Soup
>Sandwiches with Barbecued Frank Filling
>Baked Stuffed Apples

Menu 2:

>Turkey Noodle Soup
>Sandwiches with Tuna Filling
>Apple Fool

Menu 3:

>Down-Home Beef Stew
>Carrot and Celery Sticks
>Orange Raisin Muffins

BROWN BAG LUNCHES FOR TEENAGERS

Menu 1:

>Spaghetti and Meat Balls
>Tomato Salad
>Banana Pudding

Menu 2:

>Super Hero
>Ginger Peachy Salad
>Old-Fashioned Oatmeal Cookies

Menu 3:

>Crisp Cold Chicken
>Three Bean Salad
>Strawberries with Strawberry Cream
>Whole-wheat Shortbread

BROWN BAG LUNCHES FOR AT-THE-OFFICE

Menu 1:

>Creamy Corn Chowder
>Barbecue Ribs
>Bean and Pepper Slaw
>Whole-wheat Blueberry Muffins

Menu 2:

>Honest-to-Goodness Hearty Vegetable Soup
>Sandwiches with Ham and Apple Filling
>Quick Summer-Fruit Pies

Menu 3:

>Crunchy Turkey Wings
>Fresh Mixed-vegetable Salad
>Savory Cheese Biscuits
>Fresh Lemon Whip

BROWN BAG LUNCHES ON-THE-JOB

Menu 1:

>B.L.T. Double Decker Sandwiches
>Apple Apricot Medley
>Peanut Balls

Menu 2:

                    Potato and Tuna Salad
                    Chinese Cabbage Slaw
                    Cranberry Harvest Loaf

Menu 3:

                    Curried Rice and Turkey Salad
                    Pineapple Berry Salad
                    Chocolate Fruit Bars

BROWN BAG LUNCHES FOR A SPECIAL PERSON

Menu 1:

                    Triple Decker Sandwich—Oriental Style
                    Avocado Salad Dip with Cucumbers
                    Chocolate Peanutty Mousse

Menu 2:

                    The Tortilla Sandwich
                    NoBake Individual Blueberry Cheesecake
                    Vitamin C High Drink

Menu 3:

                    Country Captain Pies
                    Peanut Date Chews
                    Strawberry Cream

BROWN BAG LUNCHES FOR THE GOURMET

Menu 1:

                    Apple-glazed Lamb Riblets
                    Chinese Cabbage Slaw
                    Dilly Potato Bread
                    Apricots in Orange Sauce

Menu 2:

>Layered Chili Salad
>Onion Pepper Bread
>Dried Fruit Compote

Menu 3:

>Hearty Caesar Salad
>Stuffin' Muffins
>Oriental Fruit Salad

BROWN BAG LUNCHES FOR CALORIE-COUNTERS

The following menus are not designed to be part of a weight-reducing diet plan. Rather, they are for people who wish to eat wisely but lightly, paying attention to sensible nutrition.

You need to eat one-third of your calorie intake at lunch, so lunch should never be below 500 calories for anyone. An inadequate lunch will lead to low energy levels and poor attention spans during the rest of the work day.

If you are planning to diet or you are on a diet regimen, consult your physician. Make these menus part of your diet program only with a physician's approval.

All the menus below are based on one portion of the recipes cited in preceding chapters, and made with ingredients providing the lowest number of calories.

Menu 1:

Beef Vegetable Soup	82
Healthy Chef's Salad	330
Oatmeal Biscuit	128
Total Calories	540

Menu 2:

Borscht	84
Cottage Cheese and Fruit Salad	191
Whole-wheat Blueberry Biscuit	157
Total Calories	532

Menu 3:

Chinese Soup (omit eggs)	51
California Chicken Salad	340
Herbed Biscuit	144
Total Calories	535

INDEX

Ambrosia, New Style, 110
Apple
    and Corn Stew, Chicken, 28
    and Pork, Alternate Club Roll Sandwich, 48
    Apricot Medley, 111
    Baked and Stuffed, 111
    Drop Cookies, 130
    Fool, 112
    Nut Bread, 97
Apricot
    in Orange Sauce, 113
    Wheat-germ Pureé, 141
Asparagus
    and Egg Salad, 75
    Salad, 86
At-the-Office, Brown Bag Lunch Menus for, 150
Avocado
    Salad Dip, 86
    Salad Filling, 36

Bacon
    Cornmeal Muffins, 102
    Filling, Peanut Butter and, 40
Banana
    Brownies, 126
    Peanut Shake, 141
    Peanutty Bread, 96
    Pudding, 113
Barbecued Ribs, 58
Basic Guide to Brown Bag Nutrition, 6
Bean
    and Pepper Slaw, 88
    Black Soup, 17
    Garbanzo, Salad, 87
    Lima and Cheese Salad, 78

    Texas Red, Rice and Ham, 26
    Three, Salad, 87
    Turkey Stew, 27
Beef
    Filling, Mexican, 36
    Ribs, Deviled, 59
    Vegetable Soup, 16
Beet and Onion Salad, 88
Berry
    Salad, Pineapple, 120
    Very, Salad, 114
Biscuits
    Herbed, 107
    Oatmeal, 107
    Savory Cheese, 106
    Whole-wheat Blueberry, 108
Bread
    and Cereal Group, The, 9
    Apple Nut, 97
    Banana Peanutty, 97
    Carrot, 98
    Chili Cheese Skillet, 99
    Cranberry Harvest Loaf, 99
    Dilly Potato, 100
    Granary, 34
    Farm House Oatmeal, 31
    Oatmeal Soda, 102
    Onion Pepper, 100
    Pumpkin Raisin, 101
    Spreads, Better, 143
    Quick, and Muffins, 96-101
    Yeast, 32-35
    Whole-wheat Zucchini, 101
Broccoli Salad, Cauliflower, 90
Brownies, No-bake Super, 136
Butterscotch Apple Bars, 128
Buying the Best of Lunch

156 BROWN BAG LUNCHES

Boxes, 9
Cabbage, Chinese, Slaw, 89
Caesar Salad, Hearty, 70
Calorie Counters, Brown Bag Lunch Menus for, 152
Carrot
  and Celery Sticks with Dip, 89
  and Mushroom Sandwich, Double Decker Alternative, 47
  and Orange Salad, 90
  Bread, 98
  Cookies, Oatmeal, 128
  Wheat Biscuits, 135
Cauliflower Broccoli Salad, 90
Cheese
  and Chutney Filling, 37
  Biscuits, Savory, 106
  Rollups, Chicken, 59
  Skillet Bread, Chili, 99
Chef's Salad, Healthy, 71
Chicken
  Apple and Corn Stew, 28
  California, 72
  Cheese Rollups, 59
  Corn Dogs, 60
  Crisp Cold, 62
  Dogs, Chili, 60
  Drumsticks, Picnic, 62
  Herbed, and Wheat Salad, 74
  Liver and Mushroom Filling, 37
  Liver Filled French Roll, 44
  Pasta and Vegetable Salad, 73
  Pâté Filled French Roll, 45
  Waldorf Filling, 38
  Wings, Very Spicy, 63
Chickpea Sausage Salad, Spicy, 74
Chili
  Cheese Skillet Bread, 99
  Chicken Dogs, 60
  Chili-to-Go, 23
  Layered, Salad, 75
Chinese
  Cabbage Slaw, 89
  Soup, 18
  Vegetable Salad Filling, 41
Citrus Cinnamon Fruit Salad, 115
Chocolate
  Fruit Bars, 127
  Meltaways, No-bake, 130
  Peanutty Mousse, 114
Chowder, New England Clam, 23
Chutney Filling, Cheese and, 37
Club Roll Sandwich
  Apple and Pork, 48
  Overstuffed, 48
Cookies, 126-132
  Apple Drop, 130
  Banana Brownies, 126
  Butterscotch Apple Bars, 128
  Chocolate Fruit Bars, 127
  No-bake Chocolate Meltaways, 130
  Oatmeal Carrot, 128
  Old-fashioned Oatmeal, 129
  Peanut Date Chews, 129
  Whole-wheat Short Bread, 131
Corn Pimiento Salad, 92
Cornish Pastries, 63
Cottage Cheese and Fruit Salad, 72
Country Captain Pies, 64
Crackers and Cheese, 144
Cranberry Harvest Loaf, 99
Cucumber Salad, Crisp, 92

Date Muffins, 103
Desserts, Light Fruit, 110-123
  Apple Apricot Medley, 111
  Apple Fool, 112

INDEX

Apricots in Orange Sauce, 113
Desserts, Light Fruit (cont.)
  Baked Stuffed Apples, 111
  Banana Pudding, 113
  Chocolate Peanutty Mousse, 114
  Citrus Cinnamon Fruit Salad, 115
  Dried Fruit Compote, 116
  Fresh Lemon Whip, 117
  Ginger Peachy Salad, 119
  No-bake Individual Blueberry Cheesecakes, 116
  Orange Snow, 118
  Oriental Fruit Salad, 119
  Pineapple Berry Salad in Fresh Fruit Juice, 120
  Pumpkin Chiffon Mousse, 120
  Quick Summer-Fruit Pies, 122
  Refreshing Melon Salad, 118
  Rice Mold with Pears, 121
  Strawberries with Strawberry Cream, 121
  Very Berry Salad, 114
Dip
  Avocado Salad, 86
  for Carrots and Celery Sticks, 89
Double Decker Sandwiches
  B.L.T., 47
  Cheese and Mushroom, 47
Dried Fruit Compote, 116

Egg
  and Asparagus Salad, 76
  Rolls, 65
  Salad Filling, Deli, 38
  Scotch, 65
Eggplant Salad, Hearty, 77
Empanadas, 68

Farmhouse Oatmeal Bread, 31
Fennel Salad, 90
Fillings
  Avocado Salad, 36
  Beef, Mexican, 36
  Cheese and Chutney, 37
  Chicken Liver and Mushroom 37
Food-safety and the Brown Bag Lunch, 12
Fruit
  and Vegetable Group, The, 8
  Bars, Chocolate, 127
  Citrus Cinnamon Salad, 115
  Salad, Cottage Cheese and, 72

Ginger Peachy Salad, 119
Gourmet, Brown Bag Lunch Menus for the, 151
Granary Bread, 34
Granola Bars, 134
Green, Dark Leafy Salad with Buttermilk Dressing, 92
Green Pea and Lettuce Salad, 93

Ham
  and Cheese, Macaroni Salad, 78
  Salad and Rice, 81
  Texas Red Beans, Rice and, 26
Herbed Biscuits, 107

Italian Triple Decker Sandwich, 53

Kid Appeal, Brown Bag Lunch Menus with, 149

Lamb Riblets, Apple-glazed, 61
Leafy, Dark Green Salad with

158 BROWN BAG LUNCHES

Buttermilk Dressing, 92
Lemon, Fresh, Whip, 117
Lentil and Tomato Salad, 77
Liver, Chicken, and Mushroom Filling, 37
Lunch Boxes, Buying the Best, 9

Macaroni, Ham and Cheese Salad, 78
Meat Balls, Spaghetti and, 26
Meat Group, The, 7
Meat Pies (Mexican) Empanadas, 68
Melon Salad, Refreshing, 118
Milk Group, The, 7
Muffins, 102-108
  Bacon Cornmeal, 102
  Date, 103
  Orange Raisin, 104
  Stuffin', 106
  Toasted-wheat Buttermilk, 104
  Walnut Bran, 105
Mushroom
  Filling, Chicken Liver and, 37
  Salad, 93

New Orleans Poor Boy Sandwich, 45
New Orleans Rich Boy Sandwich, 46
Nibbles, Nutritious, Savory, 137
Nonsandwich Supersandwich, 50
Nonsandwich Supersandwich Variation, Cheese and Pineapple, 51
Nutritious Savory Nibbles, 137

Oatmeal
  Biscuits, 107
  Bread, Farm House, 128
  Cookies, Old-fashioned, 129
  Soda Bread, 102
Old-fashioned Bread, White, 31
On-the-Job, Brown Bag Lunch Menus for, 150
Onion Pepper Bread, 100
Orange
  Booster, Hot, 139
  Nog, 141
  Raisin Muffins, 104
  Snow, 118
Oriental
  Fruit Salad, 119
  Vegetable Salad, 91

Peachy, Ginger Salad, 119
Peanut
  Balls, 126
  Date Chews, 129
Peanut Butter
  and . . . , 145
  and Bacon Filling, 40
  Muffins with Cheese Filling, 137
  Peanut Butters, 136
Peanutty Bread, Banana, 97
Pies, Four Fabulous, 66
Pineapple Berry Salad, 120
Pita
  Sandwich, 54
  Vegetarian Alternative Sandwich, 55
Poor Boy Sandwich, New Orleans, 45
Potato
  and Tuna Salad, 80
  Bread, Dilly (yeast), 100
  Dilly Bread, 32
  Salad, German-style, 79
  Salad, Old-fashioned, 80
  Soup, Country-style, 19
Pumpernickel Bread, 33
Pumpkin
  Apricot Squares, 138

INDEX

Chiffon Mousse, 120
Raisin Bread, 101

Quick Breads and Muffins, 96-101

Ribs
  Barbecues, 58
  Deviled Beef, 59
Rice
  and Ham Salad, 81
  and Ham, Texas Red Beans, 26
  Curried, and Turkey Salad, 82
  Mold with Pears, 121
Rich Boy Sandwich, New Orleans, 46

Salads, Big Main-dish, 70-84
  California Chicken, 72
  Caesar's Salad, Hearty, 70
  Chef's Salad, Healthy, 71
  Chicken, Pasta, and Vegetable, 73
  Curried Rice and Turkey, 82
  Egg and Asparagus, 76
  Eggplant, Hearty, 77
  Herbed Chicken and Wheat, 74
  Layered Chili, 75
  Lentil and Tomato, 77
  Lima Bean and Cheese, 78
  Macaroni, Ham and Cheese, 78
  Spicy Chickpea Sausage, 74
  Potato and Tuna, 80
  Potato, German-style, 79,
  Potato, Old-fashioned, 80
  Rice and Ham, 81
  Tomato Mozzarella, 83
  Turkey Waldorf, 83
Salad, Single-serving, 86-94
  Asparagus, 86
  Avocado Salad Dip with Cucumbers, 86
  Bean and Pepper Slaw, 88
  Beet and Onion, 88
  Carrot and Orange, 90
  Carrots and Celery Sticks with a Dip, 89
  Cauliflower Broccoli, 90
  Chinese Cabbage Slaw, 89
  Corn Pimiento, 92
  Crisp Cucumber, 92
  Dark Green Leafy, with Buttermilk Dressing, 92
  Fennel Salad, 90
  Fresh Mixed-vegetable, 91
  Garbanzo Bean, 87
  Green Pea and Lettuce, 93
  Mushroom, 93
  Oriental Vegetable, 91
  Squash, 94
  Three Bean, 87
  Tomato, 94
Sandwich
  Fillings, 36-42
  Spreads, 145
  Super, 44-56
Sausage
  and Pepper Stew, 24
  Rolls, 68
Scotch Eggs, 65
Seafood Salad Filling, 39
Snack, Blaze-the-Trail, 138
Soups, 16-21
  Beef Vegetable, 16
  Black Bean, 17
  Borscht, 17
  Chinese, 18
  Creamy Corn Chowder, 18
  Leek and Chicken, 21
  Potato, Country-style, 19
  Tomato, Fresh, 20
  Turkey Noodle, 21
  Vegetable, Honest-to-Goodness Hearty, 20
Spaghetti and Meatballs, 26

Special Person, Brown Bag
    Lunch Menu for, 151
Spinach Power, 142
Spreads, Better Bread, 143
Stews, 22-28
    Chicken, Apple and Corn, 28
    Chili-to-Go, 23
    Country Captain, 22
    New England Chowder, 23
    Sausage and Peppers, 24
    Spaghetti and Meatballs, 26
    Sweet-sour Turkey Barbecue, 25
    Texas Red Beans, Rice and Ham, 26
    Turkey Bean, 27
Strawberries with Strawberry Cream, 121
Strawberry Cream, 139
Stuffed Jelly-roll Sandwiches, 56
Stuffin' Mufins, 105
Summer-fruit Pies, Quick, 122

Teenagers, Brown Bag Lunch Menu for, 149
Tiger's Milk, 140
Tomato
    Fresh, Soup, 20
    Mozzarella Salad, 83
    Salad, 94
    Sandwich, 52
Triple Decker Sandwich
    Italian, 53
    Oriental Style, 53
Tuna Salad Filling, 39
Turkey
    Barbecue, Sweet-sour, 25
    Bean Stew, 27
    Pineapple Filling, 41
    Waldorf Salad, 83

Vegetable
    Beef Soup, 16
    Soup, Honest to Goodness Hearty, 20
    The Fruit and Vegetable Group, 8
    Salad, Mixed-, 91
    Salad, Oriental, 91
Vitamin A Team Drink, 140
Vitamin C High, 140

Walnut Bran Muffins, 105
Wheat, Toasted-, Buttermilk Muffins, 104
White Bread, Old-fashioned, 31
Whole-wheat
    Blueberry Biscuits, 108
    Bread, 35
    Nut Bars, 134
    Short Bread, 131
    Zucchini Bread, 101

Yogurt
    and . . . , 146
    Banana Bites, 135
    Salad Snacks, 146